GW01401413

TW-138

Overleaf: *Ch. Lov-Chow's Risen Star, bred by Tim and Cheryl Lovett and co-owned by Desmond Murphy, Michael Larizza, Mr. and Mrs. Joe Vaudo and Mr. and Mrs. Lovett. "Star" is a multi-BIS/BISS winner and is six years old in this photograph. Courtesy of Dr. Samuel Draper and Desi Murphy of Liontamer Chows.*

Facing Page: *A handsome male indeed is Ch. Rebelrun Johnny B Goode, owned by Fred and Brenda Buechler, bred by the authors, Love and Bob Banghart.*

(t.f.h.)

1995 Edition

9 8 7 6 5 4 3 2 1   9   6 7 8 9

Distributed in the UNITED STATES to the Pet Trade by T.F.H. Publications, Inc., One T.F.H. Plaza, Neptune City, NJ 07753; distributed in the UNITED STATES to the Bookstore and Library Trade by National Book Network, Inc. 4720 Boston Way, Lanham MD 20706; in CANADA to the Pet Trade by H & L Pet Supplies Inc., 27 Kingston Crescent, Kitchener, Ontario N2B 2T6; Rolf C. Hagen Ltd., 3225 Sartelon Street, Montreal 382 Quebec; in CANADA to the Book Trade by Vanwell Publishing Ltd., 1 Northrup Crescent, St. Catharines, Ontario L2M 6P5 ; in ENGLAND by T.F.H. Publications, PO Box 15, Waterlooville PO7 6BQ; in AUSTRALIA AND THE SOUTH PACIFIC by T.F.H. (Australia), Pty. Ltd., Box 149, Brookvale 2100 N.S.W., Australia; in NEW ZEALAND by Brooklands Aquarium Ltd. 5 McGiven Drive, New Plymouth, RD1 New Zealand; in Japan by T.F.H. Publications, Japan—Jiro Tsuda, 10-12-3 Ohjidai, Sakura, Chiba 285, Japan; in SOUTH AFRICA by Lopis (Pty) Ltd., P.O. Box 39127, Booysens, 2016, Johannesburg, South Africa. Published by T.F.H. Publications, Inc.

MANUFACTURED IN THE UNITED STATES OF AMERICA
BY T.F.H. PUBLICATIONS, INC.

The Proper Care of
CHOW CHOWS

Love and Bob Banghart

A beautiful Chow Chow male puppy, bred by Paul and Minnie Odenkirchen of Toronto, Canada, and imported to the U.S.A. by the authors.

Contents

Introduction 7

Choosing Your Chow Chow Puppy 15

Preparing for Your New Chow Chow 25

Bringing Home Your New Chow Chow 53

Grooming 73

Standard for the Chow Chow 87

The Chow Chow's Early Years 119

To Show or Not to Show 141

The Mature Chow Chow 155

Prevention and Cure—A Healthy Life 171

Canine Behavior 233

Index 250

Suggested Reading 254

American Champion Cherie's Jubilee of Rebelrun was one of the top winning females in the U.S.A. Bred by Sherrie Harper, owned and shown by the author.

Introduction

Welcome to the wonderful world of the CHOW CHOW! I am sure that you will find this book helpful, informative, and humorous at times. If you have ever lived with a Chow Chow, you realize that *you* are owned by *them*, not the other way around. This very possessive and responsible attitude

English Champion Taibel Texas Tiger of Ukwong, a top producing sire in England, was imported to the U.S.A. by the authors.

Socialization helps the young Chow to cope with new experiences. This puppy has lovely clean eyes and a happy expression.

makes the Chow Chow an extremely loyal companion and a formidable foe to anyone wishing to harm his possessions (your home, automobile, children, etc.).

When raised as a family member, these regal, almost cat-like (most Chows even *hate* to get their feet wet!) members of the canine population can be one of the cleanest and most enjoyable breeds with whom to share your home.

The American Kennel Club (AKC) recognizes the breed as the Chow Chow, which is frequently shortened to the Chow —they are one and the same. The approved AKC breed standard defines the characteristics of the most ideal Chow Chow—both the rough coated and smooth coated members of the breed. You must bear in mind that nature does not strive for perfection, therefore no dog will exactly meet all of the specified requirements, but each member of the breed must possess enough of these characteristics to distinguish it from members of similar breeds.

The most frequently seen rough coat has a profuse coat of medium length, with a distinguishing ruff and long hair on the back of the legs and tail. The rough and smooth coated Chow Chow have a double coat — on the adult, the outer hairs are coarse and offstanding with the inner layer being soft, wooly, and thick. The smooth coat is short and dense, with no fluffy long coat on the tail, mane, or breeches. Both coat types are beautiful when well

This Chow youngster is changing from puppy coat. The dark red on his legs is the new adult coat.

tended, and the decision to purchase a rough or smooth coated Chow Chow may well depend upon the amount of time you have to devote to grooming as well as your personal preference.

The Chow Chow is considered to be a dog of medium size, with the average height of adults being from 17 to 20 inches at the withers. The ideal specimen is squarely built, with strong muscular development and heavy bones. Males are commonly larger and heavier than females, with a more

A lovely short-backed Chow puppy, this youngster grew up to be Ch. Sonlit Imagine the Duke.

abundant coat and masculine appearance. Adult females will commonly weigh from 35–65 pounds, while males may attain adult weights of 55–80 pounds. I believe the largest Chow Chow noted in documentation weighed 115 pounds—this is uncommonly large!

A beautiful square black Chow in glorious coat is hard to resist. This is Bruce and Annette Rathburn's Ch. Rebelrun Dark Oracle.

There are two unique characteristics of the breed—the blue-black pigment of the mouth and tongue, and the straight, stilted rear gait, which results from minimal angulation of the hind legs. The straight hind leg structure makes it very difficult for the Chow Chow to jump any appreciable height—even jumping into the car may be impossible. We rarely hear of a Chow escaping from the yard by jumping a fence—he is more likely to wait for an open gate!

The aloof attitude and distinguished scowl of the Chow Chow make him appear unfriendly, hence many people are wary of the breed before becoming acquainted with them. The Chow is especially aware of fear in man or animal (cats are notable examples) and will totally enjoy a game of intimidation or chase. Both males and females exhibit this ability and neutering or spaying may reduce this desire to dominate the fearful.

The cat-like aloofness and scowl distinguish the Chow from all other dog breeds. This is Ch. Rebelrun Bobby Dazzler owned by Don and Rhonda Richardson.

Rhapsody's Mister Big Shot, bred and owned by Fred and Brenda Buechler of Concord, California.

Black smooth coated Chow Chow puppy is seven weeks old.
Bred, owned, and photographed by Raymond Cadena.

Choosing Your Chow Chow Puppy

Before you begin in your search for a puppy, read as many publications as available about each of the breeds in which you are interested. If you know people who own dogs of the breed,

A young puppy and her two Siberian Husky friends pose for a holiday photo.

visit them and ask them questions. The more research you can do before purchasing your Chow, the better prepared you will be for your experience. The Chow Chow is not a dog for everyone, and it is far better to make that determination before acquiring a puppy.

WHY ARE WE DOING THIS?

There are many reasons *not* to own a Chow Chow. Examples of these are:

1. I want a dog to play fetch and chase with the kids.

The Chow Chow is not for everyone. Try to learn as much about the breed as you can to see if it's right for you. Owner, Ray Cadena.

2. I want a low-maintenance dog that will require little of my time and energy.

3. We want a dog to jog with in the ocean and to be a watch dog.

4. We want a cute puppy for the kids for Christmas.

5. I want a puppy for my fiancé mother-in-law/friend for his birthday.

6. We think we can make money breeding this kind of dog.

These are reasons commonly shared by people who call in search of a puppy. I encourage these people to give serious consideration to adopting a wonderful pet from the animal shelter, thus saving a

Select a dog whose personality best fits your lifestyle. Owned by Clif and Linda Bender.

life and at the same time being able to see the dogs and select the personality that best fits the person's lifestyle. The thought of breeding dogs as a source of income is humorous at best to the experienced Chow Chow breeder, as this

This eight week old smooth coated puppy has a lovely front and expression. He is bred and owned by Tim Malueg.

is a breed with many obstacles to problem-free reproduction. Some of the correct reasons for selecting this breed are:

1. We want a dedicated family companion, clean and well-mannered, who will require mild exercise, and not bark needlessly.

2. We have owned a Chow Chow in the past and will never own another breed!

3. We are looking for a good house dog that we can enjoy caring for and keeping his coat beautiful, possibly to exhibit in dog show conformation or obedience competition.

We find many young couples or retired couples who take great pleasure in sharing their home with this breed. They have the time to give the dog proper care yet enjoy the cat-like aloofness of the

Chow. It must be realized that a Chow who is not well socialized or raised with children should not be expected to tolerate them. The Chow will most likely see the children as intruders and his natural possessive attitude may cause an unpleasant event.

SHALL WE ACQUIRE A MALE OR FEMALE?

Once the decision has been made that the Chow Chow is the perfect dog for your home, the choice of a male or female must

Once you have decided to own a Chow, the next decision to make is whether to get a male or female. This four month old male is owned by Michael and Carol Hawke.

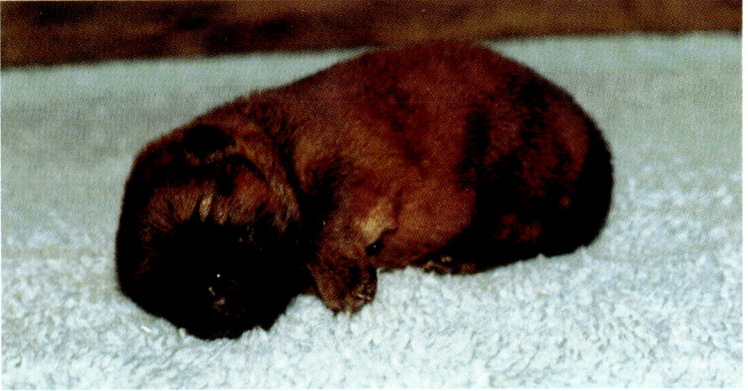

A two week old puppy at nap time.

be made. The males are larger and exhibit more dramatic characteristics of the breed, while the females are less flamboyant and more feminine (much like the lion and lioness).

The male personality tends to be more outgoing, less home-oriented, and bolder. The female is maternal, territorial, and generally quiet in nature. The female's coat is usually not as profuse as the male's, and she is smaller in stature. Both males and females are equally stubborn!

WHAT SHOULD WE LOOK FOR IN SELECTING OUR PUPPY?

The *most important* attribute to look for in

a Chow puppy is *good temperament!* The most beautiful Chow Chow in the world cannot be a friend to man if his temperament is unstable. Take time to see the dam and sire (if possible) of the puppy. They should be approachable and non-aggressive with the owner present. Do not expect them to jump up and greet

There is nothing prettier than a Chow puppy! This youngster grew up to be a top winner for Jeff and Susie Sedillos in specialty shows and a Best in Show—Ch. Rebelrun's Call to Glory.

you warmly, for the Chow is naturally aloof and reserved. The puppy should approach you inquisitively, with tail up and showing *no* aggressive tendencies. The puppy's eyes should be dry and clear, his nose should be free of discharge, and his rear should be clean and show no signs of upset stomach or intestinal problems. You should be able to play with the puppy and handle him without any display of temper. He may be timid at first, but this should disappear quickly as he becomes familiar with you and your family. It will become your

A litter of four week old puppies at Sonlit with Joshua and Rachael Hawke.

Two Chow puppies at play. Remember the most important consideration when choosing your puppy is good temperament.

job to keep the puppy well socialized, therefore selecting a puppy with a good attitude will help make your job easier and avoid problems in the future.

Your home should be prepared before the arrival of your puppy to insure the comfort of everyone.

Preparing for Your New Chow Chow

YOUR HOME

Prior to bringing your new Chow puppy home, there are several things we recommend you check in your home. The following list will provide a starting place for puppy-proofing your home and making sure that it is a safe place for your puppy:

1. The puppy should have a clean, dry area in which to sleep and play. The Chow Chow prefers to sleep on a nice, cool tile or wooden floor rather than a thick carpet or fluffy bed. You must remember, he comes with a very warm coat attached! Your expensive fluffy bed may turn up in shreds as your Chow tries to use it as a toy. If you feel that your dog needs a clean, dry place to sleep while out of doors, a low wooden pallet will make him very happy.

2. Remove all electrical cords from the puppy's reach. Many puppies are killed or seriously injured from chewing

on electrical cords.

3. If you have valuable furniture which can be damaged by puppy teeth, prepare to prevent the puppy from having access to these objects until you can train him to chew only his belongings —not yours!

4. Stairs can be dangerous for young Chow puppies. Their very straight hind legs make going up and down stairs difficult at an early age. If you have steep stairs, a pressure baby gate may be used to prevent the puppy from climbing up or falling down the stairs.

5. Do *not* encourage

Four week old Chow puppies are walking well in the whelping box. Soon they will be climbing out and ready for new experiences.

your Chow Chow to jump up on the furniture. Thousands of dollars are spent each year for veterinarians to surgically repair torn cruciate ligaments in the hind legs of Chows that were injured as they jumped to or from the furniture. If you want to sit with your Chow while you watch television or read, a nice large floor cushion may provide the safest resting place.

6. Poisonous house plants should be moved out of the puppy's reach. These plants can make a young animal seriously ill or even cause death if

Monitor your puppy's play time, especially out of doors, and make sure he has safe toys to play with.

ingested. The same is true for *all* containers of cleaning or toxic materials and mouse or rat poison. Even bags of vitamins or treats should be offered in limited amounts. I can remember the story of the critically ill puppy who ate 10 pounds of

Chow puppies just love the cool tile and will often lie with their legs extended behind them to keep their body cool.

a tasty coat conditioner while his owner was at the office. Prevent the temptation!

YOUR YARD (& POOL)

The same hints apply to your yard as well as your home and garage.

If there are areas in which your pet should not play, have the proper fencing installed *before* bringing the puppy home, and *before* an accident can occur. Pools, either fish ponds or swimming pools, are *not* safe for the Chow Chow. The dense coat of the Chow quickly becomes very heavy when wet, and this breed was not

This beautiful square puppy is proud of his "big stick" – a cardboard tube.

developed as a water dog, therefore swimming is not a natural activity. We receive many reports of Chow Chows drowned in the swimming pools of their families—what a horrible sight for an owner or a young child! A good fence around the pool is a very wise investment.

SUGGESTED EQUIPMENT
Indoor

The puppy should have a designated sleeping place—a large wire crate or air kennel can be used as a bed. As the

HOME SWEET HOME! The crate is an essential piece of equipment for travel as well as at home. Owners, Fred and Brenda Buechler.

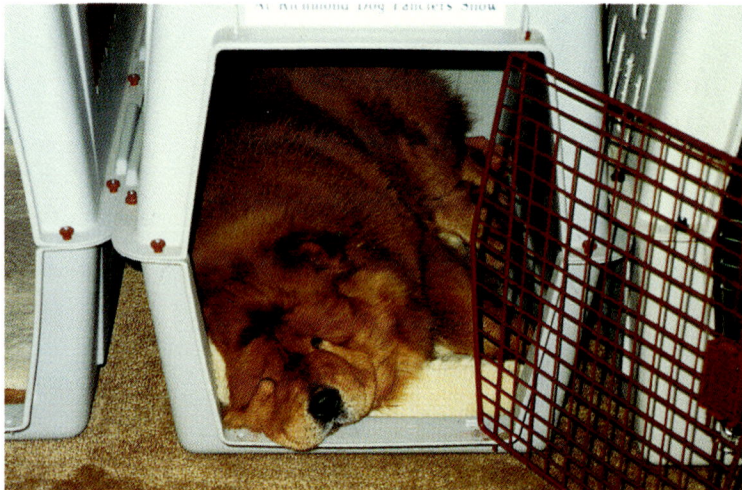

A baby gate is a great way to keep puppies confined to a single room.

Chow Chow becomes accustomed to this as his area, you will not even have to close the door to keep him in, he will automatically go in to rest. This training can be most valuable when you travel with your Chow or when you have company and need to restrict your pet's access to the party.

I have already mentioned the use of pressure baby gates to prevent access to stairs or rooms which you do not want your Chow Chow to frequent. We own

Specially designed dog bowls available at pet shops are great for traveling and at home. The top prevents the Chow's mane from getting wet when he drinks.

several of these. They are inexpensive and portable and you don't have to worry about a Chow Chow jumping over them!

Water bowls should be available in all areas where your pet will spend a lot of time. We prefer the heavy crock-type water bowls that are difficult for the puppy to turn over and cannot be destroyed by chewing. If your Chow gets his front coat wet when he drinks, you can purchase a water-hole, which is a lid with a hole in the center. The Chow requires cool, fresh water that is always available, especially in warm weather.

Outdoor

Adequate fencing is a must for the protection of your pet. The Chow Chow is a breed which *hates* to be tied, plus this will also ruin his coat by pulling hair from the mane. If you do not have a fenced area, you must be prepared to take your Chow for regular walks for exercise. Please do not turn him loose to run in the neighborhood, as he or she may stray

Adequate fencing is a must for the dog who will be outside. This is the Chow Chow family of Clif and Linda Bender.

least daily to remove debris.

A small shovel or pooper-scooper is invaluable to keep your yard tidy. You will find that once your Chow has located a favorite spot to eliminate, he will always use only that place, which makes cleanup less of a chore.

A collar and leash are essential for training and taking walks. Make sure that you purchase one that fits properly. We prefer not to use the chain collars, as they damage the Chow's mane. A good rolled leather or nylon collar works well.

A collar and leash are essential for training and taking walks. These retractable leashes are available from Hagen.

into traffic or be attacked by other dogs or neighbors!

Water bowls should also be available outdoors. The water should be changed at

FEEDING

There are many commercial dog foods that are available in the grocery store or pet store. Most of these foods are developed by companies that spend millions of dollars each year to develop the optimum nutritional formula for your dog. Your puppy will require more frequent feeding—three or four times per day on a regular basis, if possible. As the puppy grows up, the diet and frequency of feeding should be adjusted to meet his requirements, based upon activity and stress levels. Special conditions such as pregnancy, nursing, showing, or travel may require a special diet. Follow the prescribed feeding programs of the dog

A great selection of food and water dishes is available at your local pet store. Photo courtesy of Hagen.

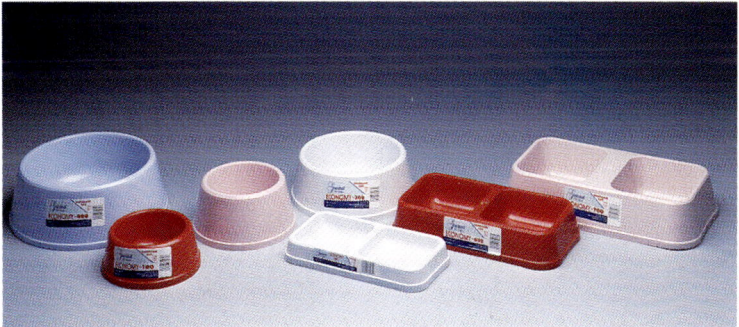

food manufacturer in order to supply optimum nutrition.

Food allergies are fairly common in the Chow Chow population, and are commonly manifested as skin problems (chewing, hot spots, rashes and hair loss). If you suspect a problem, consult your veterinarian for advice prior to adjusting the diet.

GROOMING THE PUPPY

Whether you have

The young Chow puppy begins his training for grooming as early as 4 weeks. This 7 week old is sitting quietly while his front is combed.

A complete grooming kit like this one from Hagen is necessary if you are going to groom your Chow Chow at home.

selected a rough coated or smooth coated Chow Chow, regular grooming is essential. You will need to purchase a medium-sized wire brush (called a pin brush), a metal comb with graduated separation of teeth, a nail clipper or grinder, a commercial canine ear cleaning solution, and a hair dryer. Even if you decide to have your Chow Chow groomed professionally, you will need these items for day-to-day maintenance. If you decide to do the bathing yourself, always be certain to use only shampoos developed for dogs, as other products may cause skin irritation. A medium-sized grooming table is also very nice to have, because it will make the job easier and save your back.

Puppies should be trained that grooming is a regular part of their life. It is a special time to share with your Chow.

The Chow Chow is playing in the snow with two pals. Chows are family oriented dogs and make great companions.

YOUR FAMILY AND THE CHOW

We hope that all family members were in agreement about bringing the new Chow puppy home. The Chow Chow is a family-oriented dog who, if allowed, will love each member of the household. If the puppy is introduced to children and raised as part of the family, he will readily accept and protect these children. If the Chow Chow is a family member prior to the arrival of the first child, he may initially display signs of jealousy, but as he

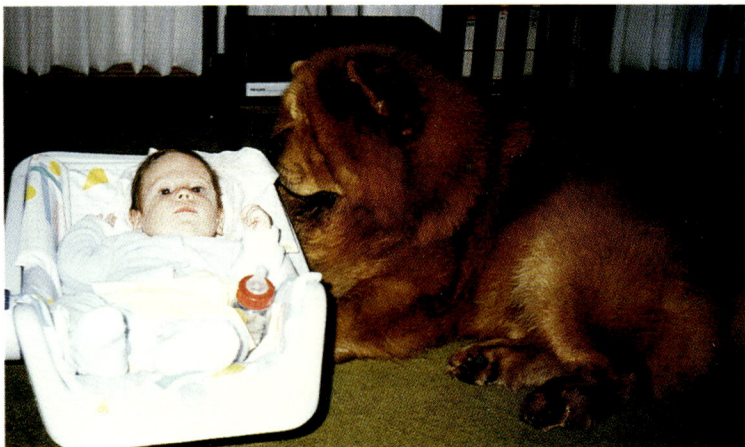

The Chow watching over the baby. Chows are very protective of their family, especially children. Owner, Gordon Van Fleet.

comes to understand that the new baby is also part of his responsibility to protect and love, he will accept the new family member. Several of our favorite children learned to walk by holding onto a Chow's mane!

Care should be exercised in allowing the Chow Chow to participate in rough play with the children. Because of his naturally protective nature, he may not understand that when one of his children begins to cry when hit by the neighbor's child, he should not intervene to protect the family member. There are many stories of parents who could not reprimand their own children if the family Chow was in the vicinity.

Children should be instructed to handle the puppy gently and with respect, as they would treat all animals.

YOUR OTHER PETS AND THE CHOW

Chow Chows have been known to share

The Chow Chow is a loving family member when raised with the children.

homes with a multitude of other animals, from horses to cats to dogs of other breeds. Once again, it is a matter of what the young puppy has been introduced to accept.

We do not recommend that male Chows or female Chows be expected to live together without a confrontation. Once a fight has occurred, there will only be many more fights, as the Chow Chow carries a grudge and *never* forgives nor forgets!

Children and Chows make the best of friends when raised together. Rachael Hawke plays with a litter owned by Michael and Carol Hawke.

Chow Chows have no qualms over sharing their home with another pet. These Chows and their Pug friend are all owned by the Hawkes.

If you want to have multiple males or females, have suitable dog runs available to keep them apart when unsupervised. A male Chow will usually get along well with a female, but even this combination has been known to have problems!

Do not expect to

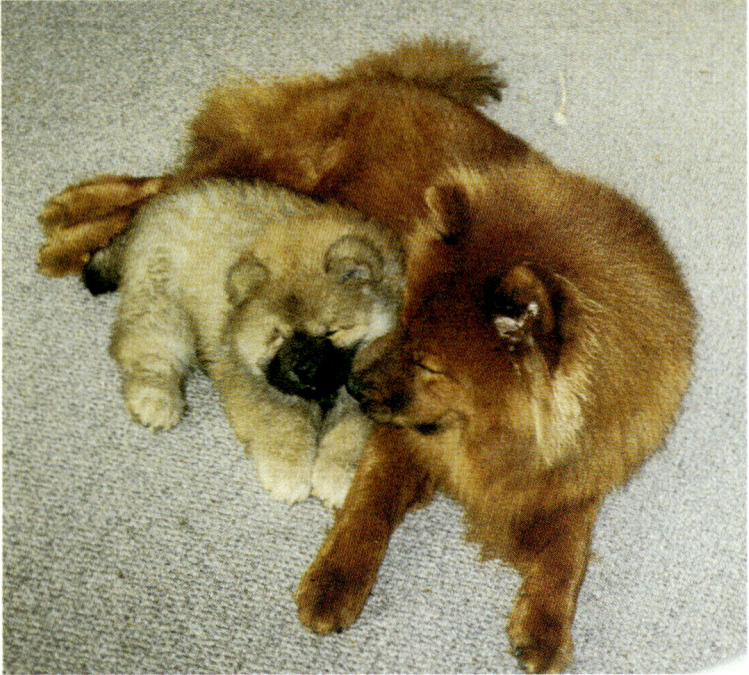

The Chow puppy and a mature Chow female (not his dam) have developed a loving relationship.

have two dominant males or females of any breed to share a home. This is usually asking for trouble. An example might be an adult male Akita and an adult male Chow— you are usually the one who will be bitten while trying to break up the fight.

YOUR VETERINARIAN

Your veterinarian should be notified that you are bringing home a new Chow Chow puppy and an initial visit should be scheduled. This allows the veterinarian a chance to examine your Chow Chow and helps to guarantee that you have acquired a healthy puppy. The veterinarian will prescribe a shot and worming schedule and will serve as an excellent consultant in keeping your Chow Chow healthy.

It is important that

These three Chows, owned by the Benders, enjoy playing in the cool grass.

you introduce your Chow to the veterinary profession at an early age. This is an important part of the socialization training and can spare you many hours of distress, as many veterinarians do not want unfriendly Chows as patients.

TRAVELING WITH YOUR CHOW CHOW

Most Chow Chows love to travel with their owners, whether it be by automobile or by air. In either case, the crate is the safest way to transport your dog. Airlines have very strict regulations for transporting dogs. These include

Ch. Ridgecrest The Floridian all ready for a trip in the van. Owners, Glee Glisson and Cindy Luoma.

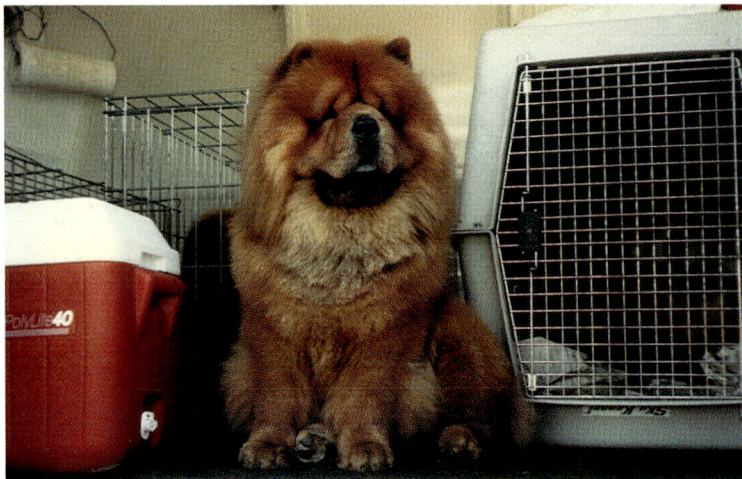

A wagonload of Chow puppies at Sonlit.

specifically approved types of crates, two water/feed dishes in the crate, and a health certificate issued by a licensed veterinarian within ten days of travel. Check with the selected airline to determine their requirements well in advance of your planned departure. Automobile travel is much less regulated and your Chow will enjoy traveling with you. The crate will usually fit snugly into the back seat or if you have a van or station wagon, into the cargo area.

This young Chow Chow male already displays the classic scowl and profuse puppy coat.

Always take a supply of fresh, cool water for your Chow Chow, even on short excursions. We recommend purchasing one of the plastic water holes, filling it half full of water, then putting it in your freezer to form a good base of ice. Just prior to travel, add more water, and instantly cold water is available for the Chow. This is also a great way to make sure that the water will last longer, as the ice melts.

Never leave any dog in a warm car without good air circulation! The Chow Chow is exceptionally inclined to suffering heat stroke and may very quickly develop breathing problems if left in a warm auto. Many hotels allow well-behaved dogs to share the room with their master, and once again, your Chow's crate can provide secure traveling for him. Always make sure that your Chow Chow is wearing a collar with your telephone number or address, even if you are only traveling to the grocery store. Should you and your Chow become accidentally separated, this will be the only way of reuniting you, unless he has one of the new identification microchips implanted

Your Chow should always wear a good collar with your telephone number and address attached in the event you become separated. Otherwise you might lose a cute puppy like this one! Photo by Isabelle Francais.

Today there are many recommended methods of identifying our dogs. Petshops carry an array of appealing I.D. merchandise. Photo courtesy of Hagen.

in his shoulder. These chips are rather new to the dog community, but are available from most veterinarians. The chips can only be located with very expensive scanning devices, which most animal shelters now have and use. However, your Chow may not ever get to the animal shelter, therefore we recommend tags in addition to the chip.

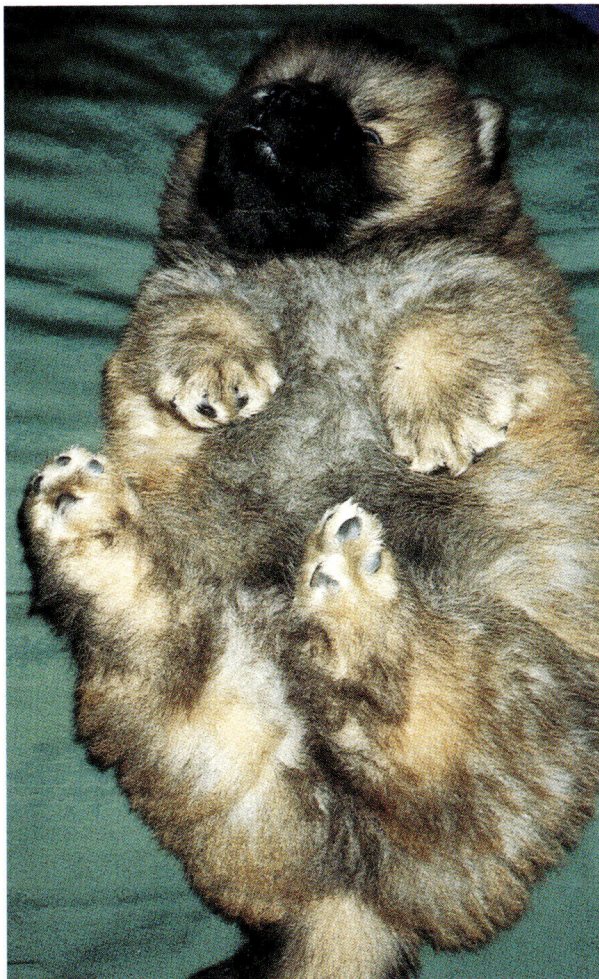

This Chow Chow puppy is totally at ease as he rests in a common puppy position.

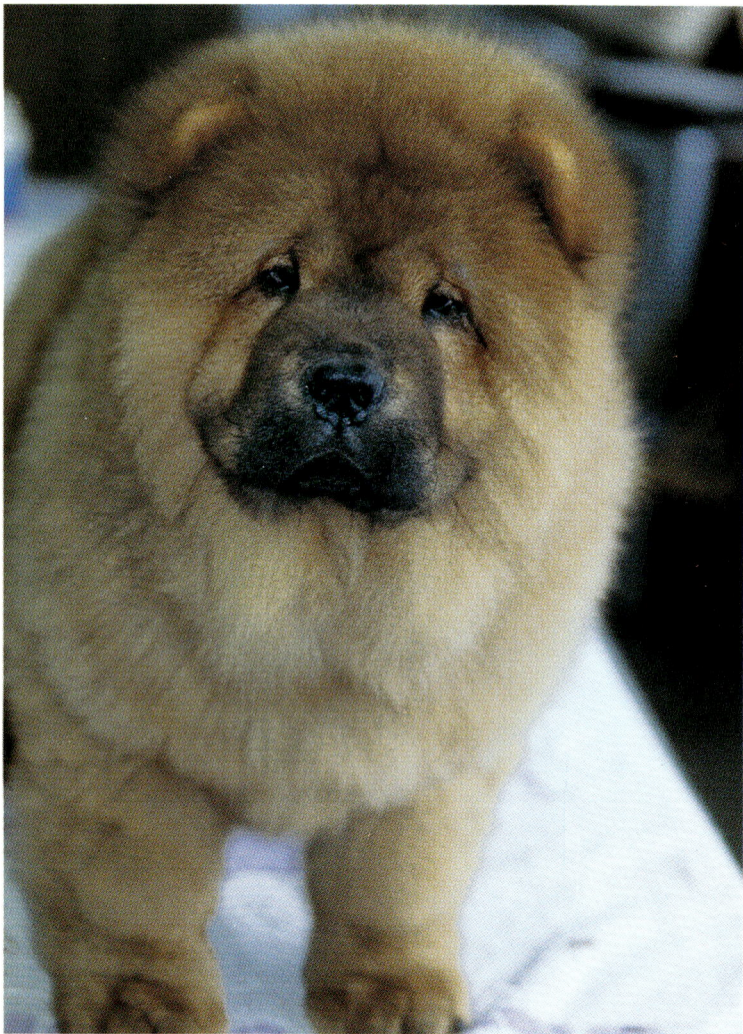

This Chow has a very feminine expression and lovely pigmentation.

Bringing Home Your New Chow Chow

THE FIRST NIGHT

You should plan to bring your new Chow Chow home at the beginning of a period of time that you and your family will all be home, such as a Friday evening after work, the beginning of a holiday weekend,

Plan to bring your new puppy home at a time when the whole family will be home, such as a weekend. This litter was bred by the Benders.

or the early part of a vacation. It is difficult for the puppy to come to a totally new environment and be immediately abandoned when everyone leaves to tend to other priorities. Planning ahead for the new arrival will make his early adjustment easier. Upon arriving home, he should be introduced to his family, his yard/exercise area, and his sleeping quarters. He should also be given fresh water and a small meal, and be allowed to fully explore the new environment. Try to avoid holding the

Introduce your Chow to his new sleeping area. The bed should be lined with blankets or towels for your puppy's comfort.

Be sure to instruct small children on how to behave with their new pet.

A Chow Chow puppy shows her toy to her friend. Bred by Fred and Brenda Buechler.

puppy. Reassure him with a friendly pat and lots of verbal praise and let him explore. If he is timid or frightened, sit on the floor near his area and speak softly to him as you extend your hand in friendship. The Chow Chow is aloof and will come to you as he gains confidence and understands that he is not in danger. *Do not* corner the puppy or grab him if he is frightened; this may result in a puppy bite that can be painful! At bedtime, take him for a short walk to eliminate, then put him in his area with fresh water in his bowl and newspaper on the floor around his bed. Once the lights are turned off, he may cry for a short period, but will settle down to sleep once he is convinced that you are not going to respond to his demands. Your puppy may have an upset stomach for the first day or so due to

Chow puppies at age 8 weeks enjoy being outdoors. The exercise pen keeps them safely confined.

stress or change of water or food, therefore he may require more frequent trips out of doors until he has adjusted.

MAN AND DOG'S BEST FRIEND—THE CRATE

One of the most useful pieces of equipment for your Chow is his dog

This 7 week old puppy is tired out from his playtime.

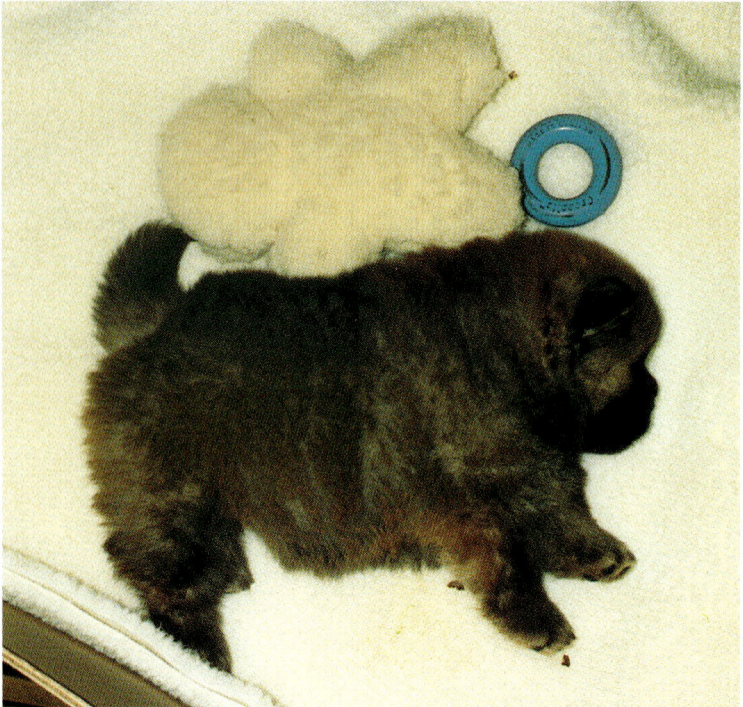

crate. It may be made of wire to maximize air flow, or it may be one of the fiberglass/plastic kennels used by the airlines. In either case, make certain that it is large enough for your dog to lie down, stand, and turn comfortably. There should be a washable pad or blanket in the crate for bedding and better footing if the crate is used for travel. The crate should become the Chow's bed, and he should be comfortable and secure in it, whether at home, in a hotel, or while driving or flying. Once your Chow Chow is accustomed to his

When your puppy plays outside, be watchful of where he goes and make sure he doesn't eat anything which will make him ill.

crate, he will be able to travel with you with a minimum of discomfort and stress.

The crate is the safest way to transport a Chow, as it prevents him from

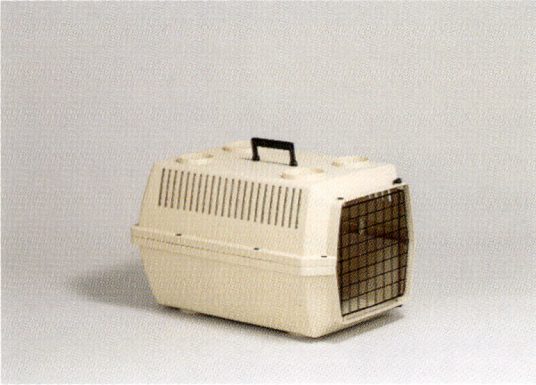

The crate is the safest way to transport your Chow, and also the ideal resting place. Photo courtesy of Hagen.

being injured if the vehicle must stop suddenly. Crates are available in a wide range of sizes. The average adult Chow will require a large or size 400 air kennel.

WHERE'S THE DOOR? (HOUSEBREAKING)

People are always amazed that the Chow Chow is extremely easy to housebreak. The clean, catlike nature of the Chow causes him to *hate* to soil his living quarters. The Chow is a very modest dog who will naturally seek the most secluded part of your yard as his spot. Once selected, that spot will only be missed in time of extreme need! A dog door is a great convenience for the Chow owner, as it allows the dog access to the yard without disturbing his owners. The young puppy should be shown to the door on his first day at his new home. Once he knows its location, he will quickly put it to use. Most Chow Chow owners report that their puppies have *never* had an accident in the house!

RULES ARE RULES!

The young Chow Chow puppy should be made aware of the rules of the house from day one. Changing rules will

A puppy's work is never done!

only confuse him. If he will not be allowed to chew on your good shoes, don't give him an old shoe as a toy. If he won't be allowed in the living room as an adult, don't bring the cute puppy in for company to visit.

Consistently enforcing the rules with the young puppy will quickly result in a well-behaved family member. The Chow Chow prefers a consistent schedule and a stable environment, so if you initiate him to

Learning to use the dog door is easy for the Chow Chow, who is naturally a very clean dog.

The typical aloof, arrogant attitude is displayed by this young Chow male, Ch. Rebelrun Back On Track, owned by Bruce and Annette Rathbun.

good habits, he will not violate those rules as an adult.

OUR SCHEDULE IS YOUR SCHEDULE

The young Chow Chow should be trained to accommodate your schedule and lifestyle. Expect to take him outside when you awaken, but don't let him determine that you

Chow Chows enjoy being part of the family. Linda Bender plays with her Chows at her Florida home.

will wake up when he wants to go out. The Chow Chow thrives on regularity—if he becomes accustomed to awakening at 5:30 a.m., he will wake you no later than 5:35 a.m. They seem to have an internal clock that is as accurate as any fine timepiece but are not aware of Daylight Savings Time.

SOCIALIZATION

Socialization is essential for the Chow Chow. Regular exposure and interaction with a variety of people, places, and events will make sharing your home and life a very pleasant experience. The Chow Chow puppy should be allowed to meet and be petted by strangers, children as well as adults. If he growls or shows signs of fear, pick him up and hold him while the stranger touches him. Should he continue to be aggressive, scold him firmly, then hold him while the stranger touches him. When he receives the attention without resistance, praise him. Young puppies will begin looking forward to guests if you allow the guests

Socialization is essential for the Chow. Interaction with both adults and children should begin early in the puppy's life.

Regular walks on the leash will enhance your Chow's personality and help him to be a well rounded family member.

to offer them treats (a piece of cheese, a dog biscuit, a toy, etc.). This reinforces the concept that your friends should also be accepted as their friends.

Regular walks on the leash and excursions away from home will enhance your Chow's personality and help him to be a well-rounded family member. A Chow left in the backyard with little human interaction can quickly become a problem at a very early age. If you do not have time to invest in socialization training, we suggest

Chows who grow up together will eventually become lifelong companions.

that you consider some other breed.

TRAINING CLASSES

All dogs should be taught obedience to some commands. No, Come, Stay, Sit, and Heel are the basics. This training, if started at seven weeks, can result in a well-trained puppy by the age of sixteen weeks—with as little as ten minutes per day of uninterrupted training time. One of our own puppies mastered the Come, Heel, Sit, and Shake commands by the age of nine weeks! The fundamental concepts for good training are: moderate repetition, consistency, immediate praise for good performance, and firmness toward misbehavior—all shared within a relationship based on mutual trust and affection. Time invested in training your Chow will be well spent, as it enhances his ability to be a pleasurable

A member of the Durman family, Rebelrun's Jack Daniels, gets a hug from his young master. What a lapful of puppy!

*Am. Ch. Rebelrun's Dark Oracle surveys the Salt River Canyon.
Owners, Bruce and Annette Rathbun.*

A dog-owner relationship based on mutual trust and affection will produce a Chow that is a pleasurable companion.

companion.

Training classes are usually offered by your local all-breed dog clubs, dog trainers in your area, or local community service groups. Many dog trainers will come to your home to give private lessons to you and your Chow.

We don't think that Chows are musically gifted, but this photo of Ch. Rebelrun's Honeybunch might convince you otherwise.

Grooming a Chow is not an easy task. If you are not up to the challenge, you may want to consider a professional groomer.

Grooming

SHALL YOU DO IT YOURSELF OR HIRE A GROOMER?

Bathing, drying, and grooming an adult Chow Chow may require from two to six hours, depending upon the amount and condition of the coat, the size of the Chow, and the type of available grooming equipment.

A good grooming table is a basic requirement in the proper care of your Chow's coat.

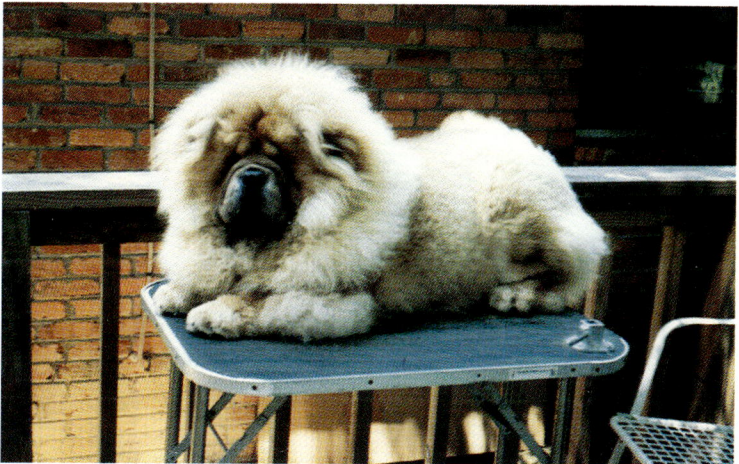

If the coat is matted, some trimming or shaving may be required. Many Chow owners prefer to spend this time with their dog, while others who have busy schedules may entrust this job to a professional groomer.

The choice to employ a professional groomer should be made only after establishing that the groomer is comfortable with and accustomed to grooming Chow Chows. We also recommend that care be taken to

Many Chow owners prefer to do their own grooming as a way to spend time with their pet. Owner, Tim Malueg.

Chows should never be placed in a hot box dryer. A warm-blowing hair dryer is a much safer alternative.

ensure that the groomer does not intend to use a hot box dryer for your Chow. Several Chows have died in these devices at the grooming parlor due to the short face and heat intolerance of the breed.

If you choose to do the job yourself, a slightly warm bath with a mild shampoo made exclusively for dogs, followed by a

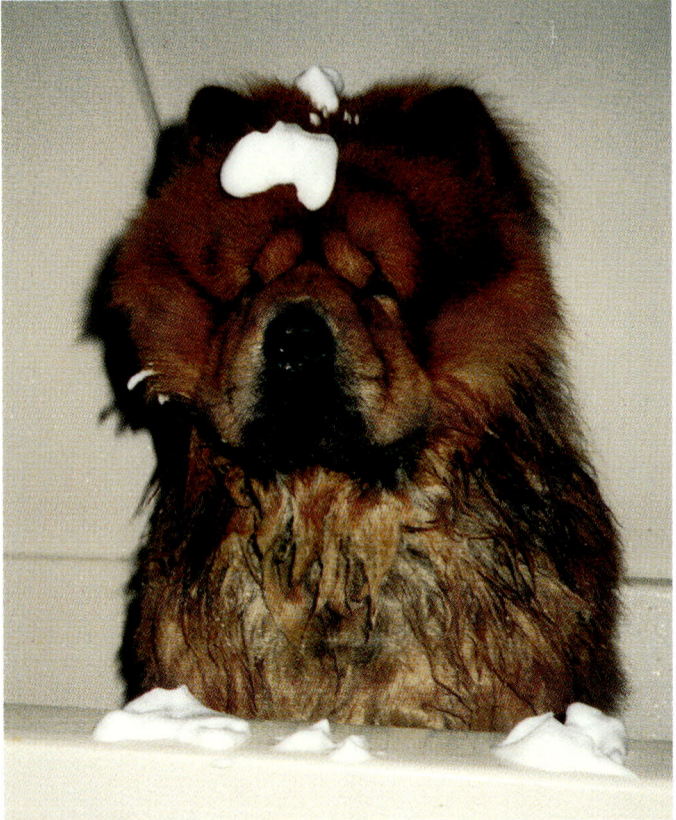

This Chow's expression leaves no doubt that bath day is not one of his favorites!

conditioning rinse, will make your Chow clean and fresh. Great care must be taken to rinse out every trace of soap or you will have problems with hot spots, which are created by the Chow licking or chewing at his skin. We suggest that you use a hair dryer to blow the coat dry after initial towel drying. If you intend to exhibit your dog in dog shows, the grooming and conditioning may be more involved. An assortment of grooming products are available for the dog owner to use at home and, when used as instructed, will do a good job of keeping your dog's coat looking great. Talcum powder is a wonderful product for a quick cleaning of the pants or feathering of the coat.

REGULAR COAT CARE

The Chow Chow should be thoroughly brushed at least three times per week. The puppy may require daily brushing, as the soft thick puppy coat is easily tangled (especially behind the

An assortment of grooming products are available at your local pet store. Photo courtesy of Hagen.

ears) and the puppy may keep his front wet by drooling. This drooling occurs while the puppy's baby teeth are being replaced with his adult teeth. This messy situation may last for a few months or a full year, until all adult teeth have matured.

The body coat and mane should be brushed forward toward the head, while the leg coat is brushed downward. The pin brush and comb are excellent tools for this maintenance. Many Chow owners like to do this grooming while the dog is lying on the floor, watching television with them. A grooming table

A nine-week-old Chow puppy waits patiently on the grooming table.

Since many Chows drool when they are warm or excited, a bib can be a useful aid in keeping the front dry.

will make the job easier, as it positions the dog at a comfortable height and helps to ensure that he stays in place for the duration of the process if you use the grooming arm attachment.

EYES AND EARS

The Chow Chow's face should be washed each morning with a

A beautiful head study of the male Ch. My-Sam's Knight in New York, bred and owned by Frank and Sandra Holloway.

warm wet cloth, paying special attention to the eyes. Any abnormal matter or tearing of the eye should prompt a visit to the veterinarian to determine the cause. The Chow Chow is one of many breeds that may be afflicted with entropion (a rolling in of the eyelashes, thus scratching the eye), allergies, and mild infections of the eye. Prompt detection and treatment may prevent the need for expensive eye surgery. If your Chow Chow is diagnosed as having entropion, please do not delay in the prescribed treatment, as this condition, when left untreated, will eventually cause blindness.

The ears should be checked at least weekly, washing them with a commercially available canine ear cleaner, and making sure there is no abnormal accumulation of dark crust or wax. Ear mites or infections may easily be treated if detected early.

THE FEET (INCLUDING TOENAILS!)

The Chow Chow's feet are catlike—tightly rounded and compact. The feet should be examined weekly and any shaggy hair should be trimmed from the

Cleaning your Chow's ears with a powder should be done regularly. Photo courtesy of Hagen.

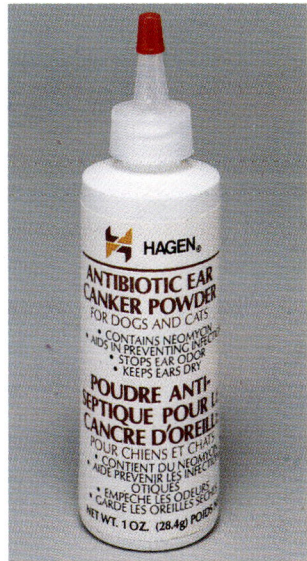

pad and the perimeter of the foot. The toenails should be kept short enough that they do not cause the foot to spread or cause the dog discomfort when moving on hard surfaces. It seems that 99.9% of all Chows *hate* to have their nails trimmed or sanded with a grinder. Some dogs become so agitated that they require a veterinarian's sedation to enable the job to be accomplished. If you start trimming your puppy's nails at regular intervals as soon as you bring him home, you may avoid

The bath was fun, but the drying will take a lot longer! A good dryer, brush and comb make the job easier.

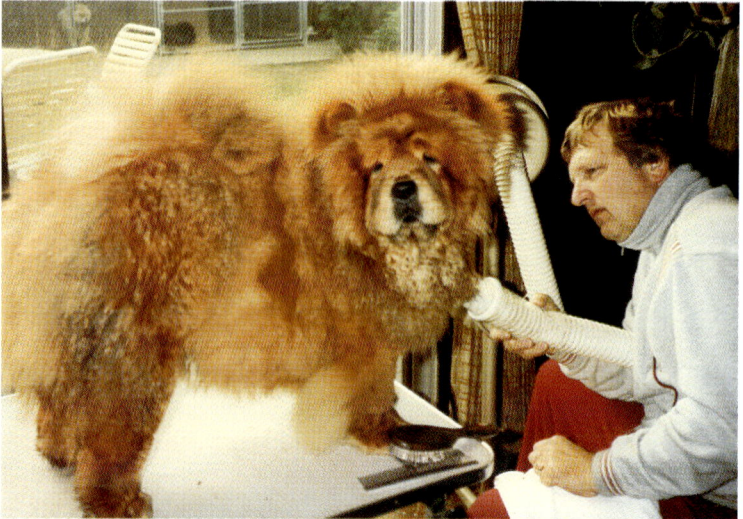

This gorgeous puppy is a picture of balance and proportion. He is bred and owned by Tim Malueg and Dale Hafner.

the difficulties. Be very careful that you do not cut into the quick of the nail (this is not easy, since the nail is usually black!), which causes sharp pain and bleeding. If this occurs, make certain that you have a styptic powder available to curtail the bleeding. Many Chows will rarely require nail trimming because they regularly exercise on concrete, thus wearing the nails down to a comfortable length. This is definitely the easiest solution to the problem! In all cases, handle a Chow's feet with caution!

An assortment of chew toys by Nylabone® are available at your pet store and aid in your Chow's preventive dental care.

TEETH

The teeth should periodically be checked for a yellow accumulation of tartar or plaque. This occurs most frequently on the molars and may cause the gums to become inflamed and sore, eventually leading to an abscess. Your veterinarian can perform a routine dental examination and schedule a cleaning if required. This cleaning will be done while the Chow is sedated and is usually a great opportunity to have the toenails trimmed and cauterized if necessary.

Bad breath is one of the symptoms of problems with a dog's teeth and should not be ignored. Other symptoms include shaking of the head, pawing at the mouth, or reluctance to eat hard treats.

A handsome red male, Rebelrun Red Alert, is well trained to stand for grooming and his photo!

Am. Ch. Rebelrun's Southern Comfort, bred and owned by the authors. His very deep set eyes require daily washing. The scowl and buttons of flesh over the eye are easily seen.

Standard for the Chow Chow

To purchase a Chow, no less to breed a Chow, you must know precisely what a good Chow looks like. Every registering organization, such as the American Kennel Club or the Kennel Club of England, adopts an official standard for the

Before purchasing a Chow, you should know what a good Chow looks like.

breed, a description of what the ideal representative of the breed should look like.

Standards, are man-made and man-remade, which is to say they change over time. These "word pictures" are subject not only to change but also to interpretation. In a perfect world, every breeder is striving for the flawless dog, which is identical in every way to the next breeder's flawless dog, which is identical in every way to the next breeder's flawless dog. In reality, however, the flawless dog doesn't exist, never has and never will. Nonetheless, breeders strive to create that "perfect specimen" and smart owners strive to find that "perfect puppy."

Read the following breed standard carefully and

There is no perfect puppy, but you should choose one which closely resembles the standard. This near-perfect bitch was sired by Ch. Rebelrun Bacardi and is owned by Vern Howard.

repeatedly. Envision every part of the dog and ask an experienced breeder or exhibitor about anything you don't understand completely.

When buying a puppy, you should know what to look for and NOT to look for. Pay close attention to disqualifications and faults. When considering gait, remember that your puppy is but a "toddler"; instead observe the movements of the parents or other relatives. Structure as well as movement are passed along from parent to offspring.

A lovely Chow puppy owned by Bruce and Annette Rathburn. His soft puppy coat is kept clean and neatly groomed.

THE AMERICAN KENNEL CLUB (AKC) STANDARD FOR THE CHOW CHOW

GENERAL APPEARANCE-

Characteristics—An ancient breed of northern Chinese origin, this all-purpose dog of China was used for hunting, herding, pulling and protection of the home. While primarily a companion today, his working origin must always be remembered when assessing true Chow type.

A powerful, sturdy, squarely built, upstanding dog of Arctic type, medium in size with strong muscular development and heavy bone. The body is compact, short coupled, broad and deep, the tail set high and carried closely to the back, the whole supported by four straight, strong, sound legs. Viewed from the side, the hind legs have little apparent angulation and the hock joint and metatarsals are directly beneath the

Though primarily a companion today, the Chow Chow was once used for hunting, herding, and pulling.

hip joint. It is this structure which produces the characteristic short, stilted gait unique to the breed. The large head with broad, flat skull and short, broad and deep muzzle is proudly carried and accentuated by a ruff. Elegance and substance must be combined into a well-balanced whole, never so massive as to outweigh his

The compact body structure of the Chow produces the characteristic short, stilted gait unique to the breed.

Ch. Sonlit Haiku at one year shows heavy bone and nice ears. Bred and owned by Michael and Carol Hawke.

This young black puppy has a pretty square muzzle, but his scowling expression is difficult to see because of his color.

ability to be active, alert and agile. Clothed in a smooth or an offstanding rough double coat, the Chow is a masterpiece of beauty, dignity and naturalness, unique in his blue-black tongue, scowling expression, and stilted gait.

SIZE, PROPORTIONS, SUBSTANCE- Size— The average height of adult specimens is 17 to 20 inches at the withers but in every case consideration of overall proportions and type should take precedence over size. **Proportions**—Square in profile and close coupled. Distance from forechest to point of buttocks equals height at the highest points of the withers. **Serious Fault**—Profile other than square. Distance from tip of elbow to ground is half the height at the withers. Floor of chest level with tips of elbows. Width viewed from the front and rear is the same and must be broad. It is these proportions that are essential to true Chow type. In judging puppies, no allowance should be made for their failure to conform to these proportions.

This Chow exhibits the square profile called for in the standard.

Proportions take precedence over size in Chow conformation. This well-proportioned Chow is owned by Michael J. Hawke.

Substance—Medium in size with strong muscular development and heavy bone. Equally objectionable are snipey, fine-boned specimens and overdone, ponderous, cloddy specimens. In comparing specimens of different sex, due allowance must be made in favor of the bitches who may not have as much head or substance as do the males. There is an impression of femininity in bitches

Perfect example of the blue tongue characteristic of the Chow Chow.

A very handsome-headed male, Ch. Rebelrun's Sir Tavish.

as compared to an impression of masculinity in dogs.

Head—Proudly carried, large in proportion to the size of the dog but never so exaggerated as to make the dog seem top-heavy or to result in a low carriage. Expression essentially scowling, dignified, lordly, discerning, sober and snobbish, one of independence. The scowl is achieved by a marked brow with a padded button of skin just above the inner, upper corner of each eye; by sufficient play of skin to form frowning brows and a distinct furrow between the eyes beginning at the base of the muzzle and extending up the forehead; by the correct eye shape and placement and by the correct ear shape, carriage and placement. Excessive loose skin is not desirable. Wrinkles on the muzzle do not contribute to expression and are not required. Eyes dark brown, deep set and placed wide apart and obliquely, of

Two happy Chows enjoy each other's company. The male is the larger of the two. Owner, Joycee Balbontin of Mountain View, Calif.

Haleakala No Ruff Stuff, a female smooth puppy. Co-owned by breeder and authors.

moderate size, almond in shape. The correct placement and shape should create an Oriental appearance. The eye rims black with lids which neither turn in nor droop and the pupils of the eyes clearly visible. **Serious**

Faults—Entropion or ectropion, or pupils wholly or partially obscured by loose skin. **Ears** small, moderately thick, triangular in shape with a slight rounding at the tip, carried stiffly erect but with a slight forward tilt.

Placed wide apart with the inner corner on top of the skull. An ear which flops as the dog moves is very undesirable. **Disqualifying Fault**— Drop ear or ears. A drop ear is one which breaks at any point from its base to its tip or which is not carried stiffly erect but lies parallel to the top of the skull. **Skull**—The top skull

The Chow head should be large in proportion to the size of the dog and proudly carried.

is broad and flat from side to side and front to back. Coat and loose skin cannot substitute for the correct bone structure. Viewed in profile, the toplines of the muzzle and skull are approximately parallel, joined by a moderate stop. The

From this angle you can see the parallel toplines of the broad muzzle and skull.

padding of the brows may make the stop appear steeper than it is. The muzzle is short in comparison to the length of the top skull but never less than one-third of the head length. The muzzle is broad and well filled out under the eyes, its width and depth are equal and both dimensions should appear to be the same from its base to its tip. This square appearance is achieved by correct bone structure plus padding of the muzzle and full cushioned lips. The muzzle should never be so padded or cushioned as to make it appear other than square in shape. The upper lips completely cover the lower lips when the mouth is closed but should not be pendulous. Nose large, broad and black in color with well opened nostrils. *Disqualifying Fault*—Nose spotted or distinctly other color than black, except in blue Chows which may have solid blue or slate noses. Mouth and Tongue— Edges of the lips black, tissues of the mouth mostly black, gums preferably black. A solid black mouth is ideal. The top surface and edges of the tongue a solid blue-black, the darker the better. *Disqualifying Fault*—The top

Rebelrun's Garfield shows the black nose and mouth which the Chow standard calls for.

surface or edges of the tongue red or pink or with one or more spots of red or pink. Teeth strong and even with a scissors bite.

Neck, Topline, Body—Neck strong, full, well muscled, nicely arched and of sufficient length to

Profile of a young Chow Chow puppy.

carry the head proudly above the topline when standing at attention. Topline straight, strong and level from the withers to the root of the tail. Body short, compact, close coupled, strongly muscled, broad, deep and well let down in the flank.

The body, back, coupling and croup must all be short to give the required square build. Chest broad, deep and muscular, never narrow or slab-sided. The ribs close together and are well sprung, not barrel. The spring of the front ribs is somewhat narrowed at their lower ends to permit the shoulder and upper arm to fit smoothly against the chest wall. The floor of the chest is broad and deep extending down to the tips of the elbows. The point of sternum slightly in front of the shoulder points. **Serious Faults**—Labored or abdominal breathing

Nine month old Ch. Sonlit All The Tea in China, bred and owned by Michael and Carol Hawke.

The Chow tail should be set high and carried close to the back. Ch. Sunny Oaks Dream Seekers Lena, bred by Ruth Kepner.

(not to include normal panting), narrow or slab-sided chest. Loin well muscled, strong, short, broad and deep. Croup short and broad with powerful rump and thigh muscles giving a level croup. Tail set high and carried closely to the back at all times, following the line of the spine at the start.

Forequarters—Shoulders strong, well muscled, the tips of the shoulder blades moderately close together; the spine of the shoulder forms an angle approximately 55 degrees with the horizontal and forms an angle with the upper arm of approximately 110 degrees resulting in less reach of the forelegs. Length of upper arm never less than length of shoulder blade. Elbow joints set well back alongside the chest wall, elbows turning neither in nor out. Forelegs perfectly straight from elbow to foot with heavy bone which must be in proportion to the rest of the dog. Viewed from the front, the forelegs are parallel and widely spaced commensurate with the broad chest. Pasterns short and upright. Wrists shall

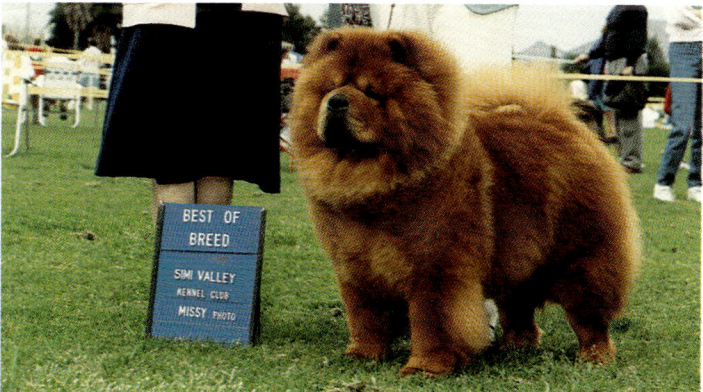

Ch. Redcloud Sylvan Eden's Tale, co-owned by Gail Riedell and the authors.

not knuckle over. The dewclaws may be removed. Feet round, compact, catlike, standing well up on the thick toe pads.

Hindquarters—The rear assembly broad, powerful, and well muscled in the hips and thighs, heavy in bone with rear and front bone approximately equal. Viewed from the rear, the legs are straight, parallel and widely spaced commensurate with the broad pelvis. Stifle joint shows little angulation, is well knit and stable, points

This Chow Chow displays the tight, round, cat-like foot that the standard calls for.

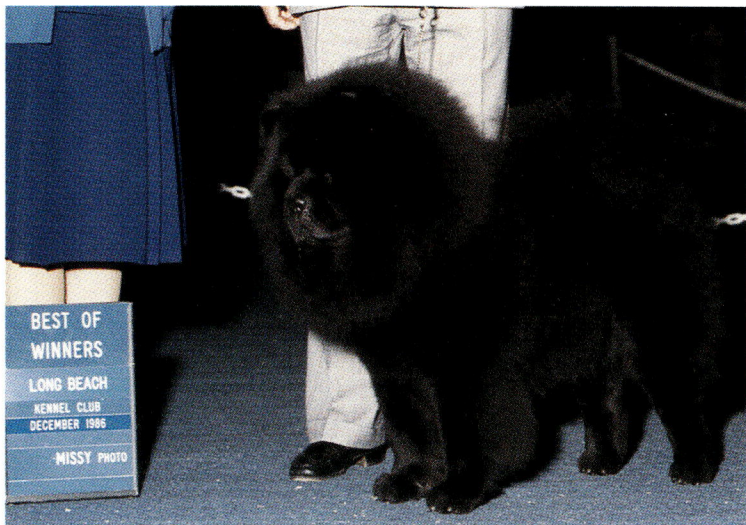

This black rough-coated Chow is Ch. Rebelruns Dark Oracle, bred by the authors, owned by Bruce and Annette Rathbun.

straight forward and the bones of the joint should be clean and sharp. Hock joint well let down and appears almost straight. The hock joint must be strong, well knit and firm, never bowing or breaking forward or to either side. The hock joint and metatarsals lie in a straight line below the hip joint. **Serious faults**— Unsound stifle or hock joints. Metatarsals short and perpendicular to the ground. The dewclaws may be removed. Feet same as front.

A black smooth Chow Chow puppy.

Coat—There are two types of coat: rough and smooth. Both are double coated.
Rough—In the rough coat, the outer coat is abundant, dense, straight and offstanding, rather coarse in texture; the undercoat soft, thick and wooly. Puppy coat soft, thick and wooly overall. The coat forms a profuse ruff around the head and neck, framing the head. The coat and ruff generally longer in dogs than in bitches. Tail well feathered. The coat length varies markedly on different Chows and thickness, texture and condition should be given greater emphasis than length. Obvious trimming or shaping is undesirable. Trimming of the whiskers, feet and metatarsals optional. **Smooth**—The smooth coated Chow is judged by the same standard as the rough coated Chow except that references to the

quantity and distribution of the outer coat are not applicable to the smooth coated Chow, which has a hard, dense, smooth outer coat with a definite undercoat. There should be no obvious ruff or feathering on the legs or tail.

Color—Clear colored, solid or solid with lighter shadings in the ruff, tail and featherings. There are five colors in the Chow: red (light golden to deep mahogany), black, blue, cinnamon (light fawn to deep cinnamon) and cream.

All acceptable colors of the Chow Chow are judged on an equal basis.

Acceptable colors to be judged on an equal basis.

Gait—Proper movement is the crucial test of proper conformation and soundness. It must be sound, straight moving, agile, brief, quick and powerful, never lumbering. The rear gait short and stilted because of the straighter rear assembly. It is from the side that the unique stilted action is most easily assessed. The rear leg

Proper movement is a crucial test of conformation. The puppy's movement should be sound, but don't expect too much too soon.

moves up and forward from the hip in a straight, stilted pendulum-like line with a slight bounce in the rump, the legs extend neither far forward nor far backward. The hind foot has a strong thrust which transfers power to the body in an almost straight line due to the minimal rear leg angulation. To transmit this power efficiently to the front assembly, the coupling must be short and there should be no roll through the mid-section. Viewed from the rear, the line of bone from hip joint to pad remains straight as the dog moves. As the speed increases

Though lacking in speed, the Chow has excellent endurance due to efficient leg structure.

the hind legs incline slightly inward. The stifle joints must point in the line of travel, not outward resulting in a bowlegged appearance nor hitching in under the dog. Viewed from the front, the line of

A family portrait of the Sonlit Chows, bred and owned by Michael and Carol Hawke.

bone from shoulder joint to pad remains straight as the dog moves. As the speed increases, the forelegs do not move in exact parallel planes, rather, incline slightly inward. The front legs must not swing out in semicircles nor mince or show evidence of hackney action. The front and rear assemblies must be in dynamic equilibrium. Somewhat lacking in speed, the Chow has excellent endurance because the sound, straight rear leg provides direct, usable power efficiently.

Temperament— Keen intelligence, an independent spirit and innate dignity give the Chow an aura of aloofness. It is a Chow's nature to be reserved and discerning with strangers. Displays of aggression or timidity are unacceptable. Because of its deep set eyes the Chow has limited peripheral vision and is best approached within the scope of that vision.

Summary—Faults shall be penalized in proportion to their

This regal male, Ch. Jonel's Track Mactavish, was an important sire and show dog for the author.

deviation from the standard. In judging the Chow, the overall picture is of primary consideration. Exaggeration of any characteristic at the expense of balance or soundness shall be severely penalized. Type should include general appearance, temperament, the harmony of all parts, and soundness especially as seen when the dog is in motion. There should be proper emphasis on movement, which is the final test of the Chow's conformation, balance and soundness.

In judging the Chow, the overall picture is of primary consideration. This black Chow is Ch. Rebelrun's Stratofortress.

This Chow puppy exhibits a lovely square muzzle. The black coloring will change to red as he matures.

This little Chow Chow female shows off her new scarf and her pretty blue-black tongue.

The Chow Chow's Early Years

GROOMING IS DIFFERENT NOW!

You will notice a difference in your Chow Chow's coat as he gets older. The texture and possibly the color will change. This begins at about four months of age and may continue until the dog is almost two years old. The fluffy, wooly puppy coat will be

The texture and possibly the color of your Chow's coat will begin to change at around four months of age.

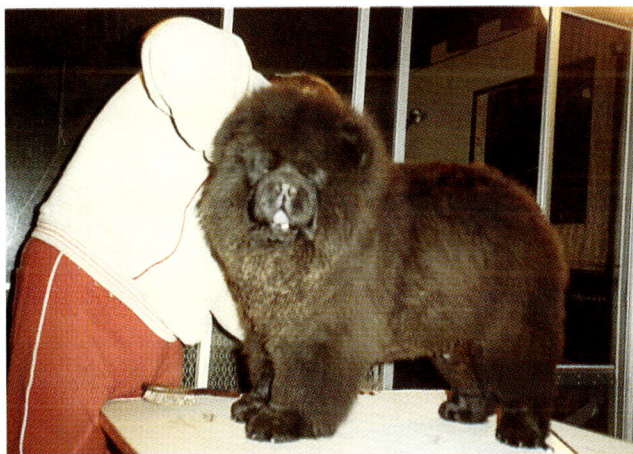

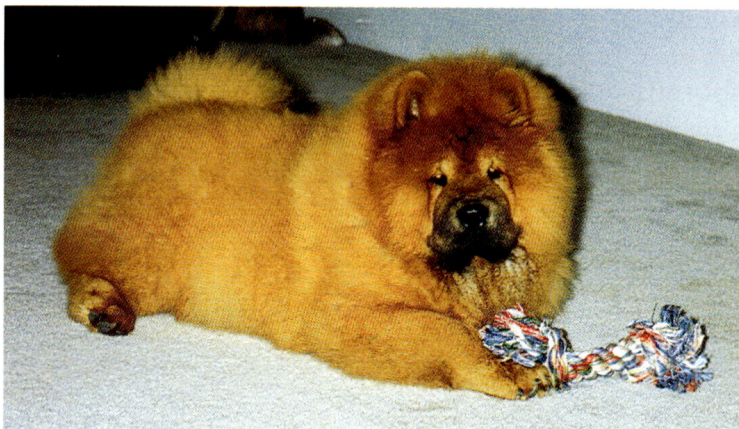

Safe chew toys such as Nylafloss™ should be made available to your Chow for his dental health.

replaced with coarse, straight, shiny guard hairs. These will become the adult's outer coat layer. In red Chows, this new coat may be significantly darker than the puppy coat. The adult coat is easier to care for, is longer, will not mat as easily, and will look groomed for a longer period of time than the puppy coat. There should be a thick, wooly undercoat close to the skin. This combination is referred to as double coated. Many of the Arctic breeds are recognized as being double coated adults.

STAYING HEALTHY

Your veterinarian should be recognized as a friend who helps to care for your Chow and who will prescribe regular schedules for examinations and health maintenance.

SHOTS AND TESTS

Your puppy will require a rigorous schedule of puppy inoculations to protect him from the many diseases which he may be exposed to during his early days. Once

At one year, the female Chow will begin to show a feminine face with more expression starting to develop.

his body has built immunities to these illnesses, annual booster shots should be administered for continued protection. Your veterinarian should request that you have your dog tested for worm infestation at least annually. Internal parasites can cause your Chow Chow to look unhealthy and have intestinal upsets. Some parasites, such as heartworm, can be lethal if not treated promptly.

Constant chewing, scratching and hair loss should be quickly evaluated and appropriate treatment administered before more serious skin infections can erupt. Skin problems may

This young female, Mishka Sweetpea of Rebelrun, has a feminine, open face.

Ch. Rebelruns Peppermint Twist enjoys time outside with her nephew Robinhood, sired by Stratofortress.

be related to many causes—fleas, food allergies, environmental allergies, or hormonal imbalance. Once again, your veterinarian will be your best source of assistance.

OFA (ORTHOPEDIC FOUNDATION FOR ANIMALS)

The Orthopedic Foundation for Animals is a registry service available to all dog owners to evaluate hip and elbow radiographs for signs

After lunch and a nice game of tag, this young Chow enjoys relaxing.

of hereditary disease. X-rays may be submitted by your veterinarian and will be processed and reported within four to six weeks.

Your Chow Chow should be x-rayed prior to making any decision to breed, or if you detect any abnormality in movement, difficulty in standing or sitting, or stiffness. Once your Chow is two years old, he may have radiographs taken and submitted for OFA Certification If the radiologists see no signs of hereditary disease, they will issue your Chow Chow a certificate and OFA Number. This information is important, especially for dogs who will be bred. The OFA number will appear on any AKC-certified pedigree in which your Chow appears, to indicate that your dog is free of abnormality of the hips and elbows.

DYSPLASIA

If your Chow Chow does not pass his OFA Certification and is found to be afflicted with either hip or elbow dysplasia, the report will indicate the severity of the case. It has been reported that 30 to 50 percent of Chow Chows do not pass this examination. This is

Once your Chow has reached two years, he should have radiographs taken for OFA Certification. Pictured, Ch. Redcloud Sylvan Eden's Tale.

Love Banghart with two favorite Chows, Ch. Jonel's Track Mactavish and Ch. Cherie's Jubilee of Rebelrun.

why it is important to purchase your puppy from a conscientious breeder who has his Chows certified prior to breeding. Since it is commonly believed that dysplasia is a hereditary disease, your chances of obtaining an unaffected puppy will be increased.

Your veterinarian will work with you in designing a program to keep your Chow Chow comfortable and help him to maintain a long and happy life. Some dysplastic Chows will never show signs of pain or lameness; others may require occasional medication. Severe cases will usually require surgical repair. In any case, your Chow Chow should be neutered or spayed and not used for breeding if he does not pass this certification.

SHALL WE BREED OUR CHOW CHOW?

The question of breeding your Chow Chow will probably come to mind in the early months of ownership. If you have no intention of even considering this option, you should make arrangements with your veterinarian to have

Young Chow Chows love to play in the snow!

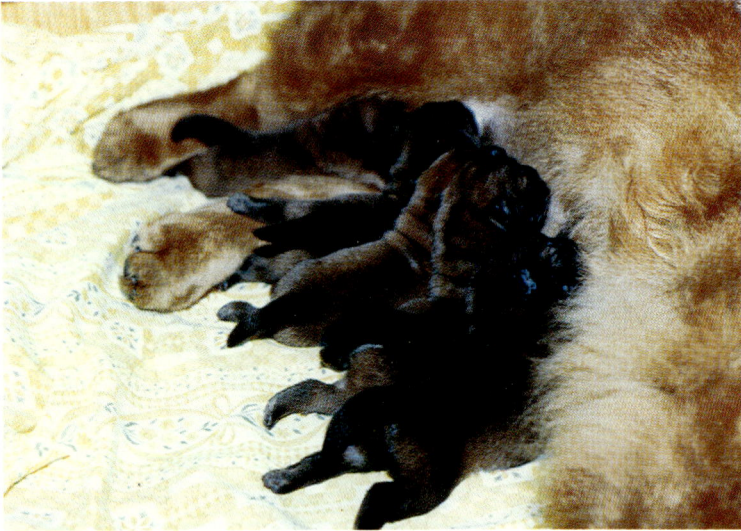

A number of important factors must be considered before you decide to breed your Chow Chow. These pups are five days old.

your pet neutered or spayed at about six months of age. The decision to breed your Chow Chow should only be made after the following questions have been answered:

Does your Chow have a good, non-aggressive temperament?

Has your Chow been certified by a veterinarian to be free of hereditary eye problems and been x-rayed for hip dysplasia?

Do you have the time and money to properly whelp and raise a litter of puppies if you own a female? Are you prepared to keep the puppies until a suitable home is found for each one?

Have you researched your Chow's pedigree to discover the important positive and negative characteristics that the puppies may inherit?

Do you have a veterinarian who is skilled in Caesarean

Be sure to research your Chow's pedigree for all positive and negative characteristics before breeding.

sections and breeding techniques?

Have you had your Chow evaluated by a qualified breeder to correctly assess his or her individual strengths and weaknesses? This evaluation will help you in selecting a mate that complements your Chow.

Have you contacted other Chow Chow breeders to discuss the available mates for your Chow and the costs involved?

A very pregnant Chow waits for the big day.

A breeder has a responsibility to the new owner. It is expected that a written guarantee of the puppy's health and quality be given.

Are you prepared to give a written guarantee of the puppies' health and quality, and refund purchase prices if there are problems?

If the answer to ALL of these questions is not yes then you should seriously consider having your Chow neutered or spayed and enjoy loving him as a companion. If you decide to breed your Chow Chow, he or she

Ch. Rebelrun The Californian (bred by the authors) has won in the U.S., Holland, and South America.

should preferably be past the age of two years and should not be older than seven years. This is the optimum age for successful breeding to occur.

SPAYING/NEUTERING

If you have decided not to breed your Chow

Chow, or if your Chow has been bred and will not be bred again, you should have him spayed or neutered. Many health problems, including cancer of the reproductive system, can be avoided by having this safe, simple procedure performed; this saves your pet from much suffering and you from expensive veterinary bills. The spay/neuter procedure can be performed as early as six months of age and at any age after that. The procedure may require overnight hospitalization, but

Many health problems can be avoided by having your Chow spayed or neutered. This procedure can take place anytime after six months.

your Chow Chow will recover very quickly from the operation.

SOCIALIZATION AGAIN—THE PROBLEM CHOW CHOW

The Chow Chow must be allowed to participate in family activities, introduced to people and activities, and treated as part of the family if he is expected to maintain a friendly, accepting attitude. If the Chow is left in the backyard, excluded from outside influence,

Santa Claus brings Chow toys too! Rebelrun's Teddy MacTyke, owned by Gene and Eileen Baldi, enjoys the Christmas season.

The socialized Chow is a joy to own. Rob-Loi Emperor of Rebelrun is a "Gentleman Chow" owned by Lois Burk.

he will soon become a recluse. His aloof nature will allow him to become self-sufficient, a "loner" who will accept your attention and adore only you. This antisocial behavior can quickly evolve into an attitude of intolerance to change and a dislike or distrust of strangers. The Chow Chow with this attitude, combined with aggression, is a serious problem. He

Socialization that begins very early in the Chow puppy's life will ensure a friendly adult.

A dog show is a great place for your Chow to develop social skills.

When Linda Bender feels ill, her Chow Chows assume their role of guardians.

cannot be trusted with your visitors, the veterinarian or groomer, or put in any social environment. It is almost impossible to enjoy the companionship of such a Chow. With careful handling and training, and a great deal of time and patience, this condition can be reversed; but few people have the time or energy to invest in this type of reformation. This is why we stress early and continued socialization, with a great deal of human contact and participation in family activities.

A beautiful Chow female, Rebelrun Arabella.

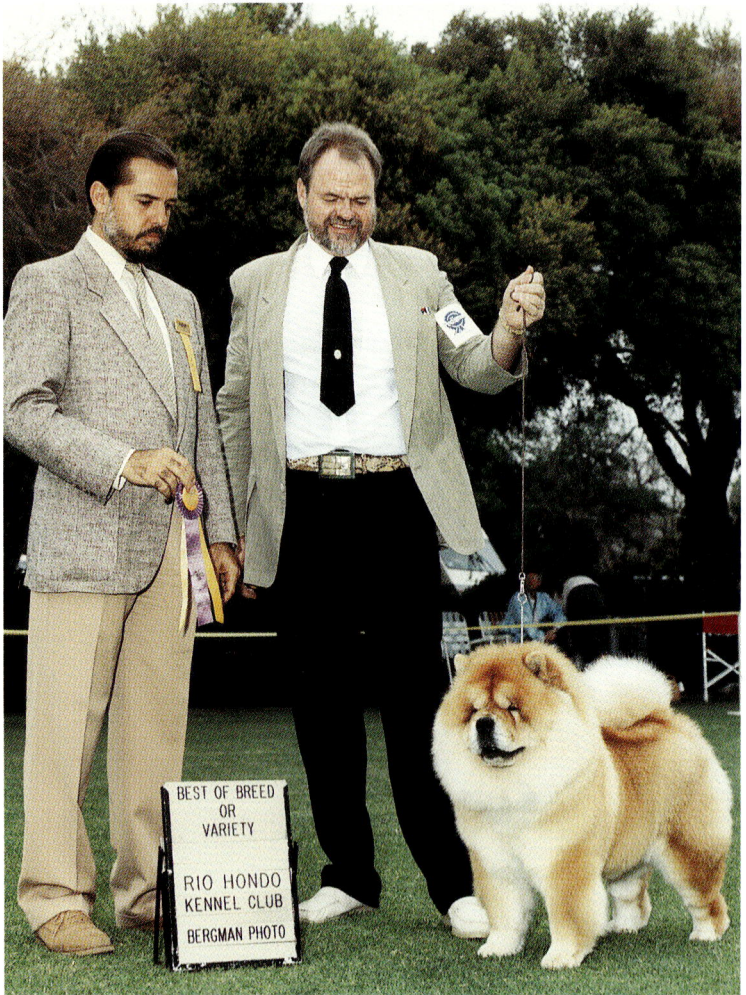

Ch. Chowlamar's Ravishing Ruby, bred and owned by Roy and Judy Bailey, was one of the top winning bitches of the early 1990s.

To Show or Not To Show

CONFORMATION

For anyone who has purchased a purebred Chow, the thought of exhibiting the dog in conformation competition is natural, since the Chow Chow is such a noble, impressive animal. If you purchase your puppy directly from a breeder, you should discuss the possibility

Showing at AKC shows can be fun! The author with her Ch. Cherie's Jubilee of Rebelrun wins at a national Chow Chow show.

BIS, BISS Ch. Rebelruns Stratofortress.

of showing your Chow with the breeder and have the breeder point out to you the outstanding breed qualities of the individual puppy or the attributes (faults) which may hinder your Chow's success in competition. These qualities and faults

Ch. Bearden's Mountain Man, bred by Harry and Lucille Gebney. Owned by breeders and authors.

Puppies have their own separate competition and judging at dog shows.

are based upon the AKC standard for the breed. The price you pay for your puppy will depend upon the breeder's evaluation of the quality of the puppy if the breeder has been involved in dog show competition.

If your goal is to have a Chow Chow worthy of attaining a championship title, you should obtain and research the puppy's pedigree. A three-generation pedigree that contains no champion ancestors is unlikely to produce that big winner that you are desiring. In general, the more champion ancestors a dog has, the higher the chances of his inheriting the attributes of a champion.

Ch. Rebelruns Dreamer for Sal Mae as a pup, now a Group winner. Sire: Ch. Jonel's Track Mactavish. Dam: Ch. Justameres Blu-Min-Rose.

An important point to remember is that there has never been a perfect dog, of any breed, born. Every dog, and of course every Chow Chow, has faults. The amount of love and companionship a dog provides has nothing to do with the standard, his faults, or his success at dog shows—he deserves your kindness and caring. In conformation competition, each dog is compared to the

This lovely Chow is getting some last-minute preparation before the big show.

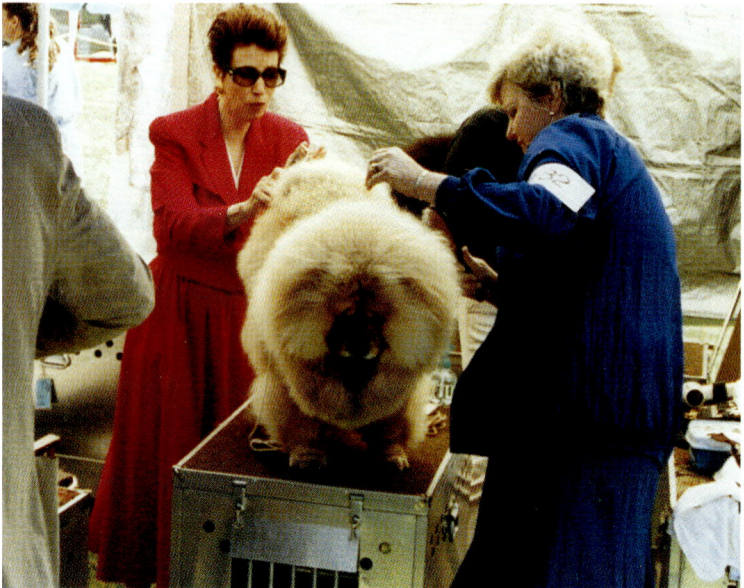

Ch. Rebelrun's Jessica, a beautiful black Chow, with the author.

AKC standard for the Chow Chow. The judge makes his awards to the Chow Chows that most closely conform to the published standard. The Chow is also expected to be well behaved and to allow the judge to examine him without any display of aggression or shyness.

The 1988 National Stud Dog Class.

In conformation competition, each dog is compared to the AKC standard for the Chow Chow. Ch. Rebelruns Amberosia.

This puppy won Best Puppy at a puppy show while in early training for Glee Glisson and Cindy Luoma.

OBEDIENCE

Obedience competition is a wonderful opportunity for you to show the world how well you and your Chow Chow work as a team. There are not many Chows Chows in obedience competition, since they are very smart, are easily bored with

BISS, BIS Ch. Rebelruns Stratofortress.

The author teaches one of his puppies to stay and stand. Two of the basic commands to teach your Chow.

repetitive exercises, and are very stubborn. This does not make an obedience title an impossibility, but does make it a title of which you can be extremely proud. We think that it shows that the Chow Chow is not only beautiful, but smart too!

Obedience competition is an excellent way to show off your Chow's intelligence. Pictured, Ch. Rebelruns The Californian.

Ch. Redcloud Sylvan Eden's Tale, co-owned by the authors.

The Mature Chow Chow

THE BEST YEARS

We feel that the most enjoyable years with your Chow Chow are those of maturity (ages three to seven). Puppy training has been completed, the Chow has developed into a mature male or female, and is physically in top condition. Your dog has become an important member of

The mature years (age 3 to 7) are the most enjoyable years of your Chow's life.

the family, who knows the household schedule, family and friends, and routine trips. He or she may have produced a litter of puppies, attended training classes, competed in dog shows, and traveled to many places with your family. Your Chow Chow is one of your most enjoyable companions.

These are the years that you can enjoy sharing your Chow in community pet fairs, therapy programs for the elderly, and public educational

A family portrait—the authors with Ch. Jonel's Track Mactavish and Ch. Cherie's Jubilee of Rebelrun.

Rebelrun's Jenny Linn enjoys some quality time with her puppies.

programs. The well-socialized Chow Chow attracts attention because of his beauty and regal attitude. Your dog can become a good ambassador for the breed. He can be an example to illustrate that all Chow Chows are not aggressive, nasty members of society. The rewards of your proper care and training come with this maturity.

SHALL WE GET ANOTHER DOG? ANOTHER CHOW CHOW?

This is usually the time when you and

A well-socialized Chow attracts attention because of his beauty and regal attitude. This fluffy female is Rebelrun's Amber Rosia.

your family may consider getting a companion for your Chow. Perhaps a new puppy will provide the exercise and entertainment that your Chow enjoys and will allow your family to use the experience gained in raising the adult!

Your new puppy should be non-aggressive in nature, compatible in size, and of the opposite sex to your Chow, even if your Chow is neutered or spayed.

These considerations will help to eliminate the chances of a confrontation between the two dogs as the newcomer matures.

Introduce the new dog as a gift to your Chow, helping the Chow to understand that this is another family member for which he is responsible. Care must be taken to ensure that you do not create a situation of jealousy by showering affection on the new dog and ignoring your Chow Chow. If your new dog is an adult, be

Once your Chow has matured, you may consider getting a companion for him. Here Clif and Linda Bender's Chows play in the backyard.

Care must be taken not to create a situation of jealousy when you acquire another Chow.

especially careful to supervise all early interaction. Be careful at feeding time to make sure that the dogs are spaced apart and do not create competitive situations over food, affection or toys.

THE GERIATRIC CHOW CHOW (AGE SEVEN)

The older Chow Chow is wise, dignified, and one of the most enjoyable of companions. If his health and grooming are well maintained, these years will be a

Showing is a great way to build a long lasting relationship between you and your mature Chow.

The average life span for the Chow is 8-10 years. Rhapsody's Mister Big Shot, owned and bred by Brenda Buechler.

joy to share. The average life span of the Chow Chow is eight to ten years, although the well-cared-for Chows have been known to live for up to 16 years.

DIET AND EXERCISE

Your Chow Chow will become less

active as he ages, and his diet should be adjusted accordingly. Many of the pet food companies now offer less active dog foods for the geriatric dog. These offer good nutrition with fewer calories. Treats should be restricted and the amount of food monitored to ensure that your Chow Chow does not become overweight.

If health and grooming are well maintained, you should enjoy a long life with your Chow. Owners, Jean and Tony Larson.

Regular moderate exercise, whether it be walks in the evening or short games of ball-chasing, can be beneficial.

PROBLEMS OF AGING

The Chow Chow may live to be 12–16 years of age if given proper care. Common problems of aging are blindness, deafness, cancer, arthritis, and occasional indigestion. Kidney failure seems quite common in dogs who have been on high-protein diets. Once again, your veterinarian will be your best consultant in the control and management of these conditions.

Your Chow will become less active as he ages, and his diet should be well monitored as his activity decreases.

The mature Chow is wise, dignified, and an enjoyable companion. Rebelrun Teddy Mactyke, owned by Gene and Eileen Burington-Baldi.

DIGNITY—THE QUALITY OF LIFE

As your Chow Chow ages, you may notice changes in his habits. His appetite may vary, and he may begin to lose his hearing and eyesight. Bladder control and

Ch. Rebelrun's Annabelle Li, owned and loved by Gloria Glisson and Cindy Luoma, poses for her portrait.

regularity may become problems, especially for the house dog.

Remember that the Chow is by nature a very clean and regal animal and he should be allowed to maintain his dignity in old age. If the day comes that this dignity is compromised by failing health, it is your responsibility to make the correct decisions for recovery or to make arrangements for

The author and one of his Champions at a dog show. It is important to have your Chow well trained and groomed for AKC shows.

BIS, BISS Ch. Rebelrun's Stratofortress.

euthanasia. This is never an easy decision, and your veterinarian will be your best advisor. It is very difficult to love your Chow Chow enough to let him go when the time has come, but his quality of life should be important to all concerned.

Ch. Sonlit Imagine The Duke.

A lovely square female in full puppy coat. Am. Ch. Lionheart Whirlwind at 4 months.

Prevention and Cure— A Healthy Life

Every owner hopes that his dog will live a long healthy life. Nowadays, this desire is enhanced through careful selection of puppies and breeding animals, modern technology and veterinary care and the family's care and concern—all of which aid in prevention and cure.

Dogs today are so much more fortunate than their ancestors. Regulations which were originally passed to protect property, livestock and humans actually ensure a dog's safety as well. Licenses and the accompanying taxes provide shelters for lost or abandoned animals, and a tag may prove to be a lifeline to home.

Modern technology has helped ensure that our dogs live a long healthy life.

Because leashes and confinement are now required by law, fewer families allow Rover to rove, and have his life ended by a bullet or highway traffic.

Many diseases commonly fatal in the early to mid-1900s are now prevented through inoculation. An old-time exhibitor understood that if he took his dog to enough shows, the animal would contract distemper sooner or later. It was common to lose entire litters to

Around the turn of the century, many active show dogs contracted fatal diseases which are now prevented through inoculation.

Universal vaccination has almost completely eliminated distemper from the dog world. Ch. Cheries Hank of Rebelrun.

the dread disease, which plagued canines for hundreds of years. Now, thanks to nearly universal vaccination, most breeders have never even seen a case.

As recently as 1978, parvovirus swept the canine world, decimating kennels.

Responsible health care begins the moment you acquire your puppy. This is Rebelrun's Call to Glory at five months.

As with all diseases, it was the very young and the very elderly dogs that succumbed in great numbers.

Thanks to modern research laboratories and the pharmaceutical companies, this time within two years a preventative vaccine was available.

GENERAL MEDICAL CARE

Before a puppy is sold, he should have received at least one full set of inoculations, protecting him from distemper, hepatitis (adenovirus), leptospirosis, parainfluenza and parvo. Many breeders vaccinate against corona virus and bordatella as well. Among the puppy's stack of official papers

Chows and snow go together! This young male is having fun in his first winter.

New kids in town! A puppy should receive his first full set of inoculations before sold.

that are turned over to the expectant parents should be a list noting the ages when additional shots will be needed. Although the schedule varies from breeder to breeder, or one veterinarian to another, the following is an example: six weeks—combination DA2PP & Cv; nine weeks—parvo; twelve weeks—combination; sixteen weeks—parvo and rabies.

Before the puppy goes to his new home, he should be examined by a veterinarian and pronounced healthy and free of major congenital defects. Most bite, eyelid, testiculate, cardial and esophagael problems can be detected before eight weeks, as can luxated patellas and open fontanels. From that point on, it's up to the new owners to continue examinations and veterinary care to keep him healthy. Routine health care, of course, includes yearly vaccinations and heartworm checks, followed by administration of the preventative.

Breeders have puppies fully examined by a veterinarian and pronounced healthy before they go to their new home.

GROOMING

Even shorthaired dogs need grooming. Brushing, combing, occasional bathing, nail trimming, as well as teeth and ear cleaning, help keep him in good condition. In addition, these sessions are ideal times to check him for any lumps, sores, rashes, parasites or other external signs of a health threat.

Brushing and combing the hair eliminate painful mats, as well as

Three day old Chow puppies snuggle to keep warm.

Socialization and emotional well-being are just as important as physical condition for the health of your Chow.

stimulating the natural oils and hair growth. Regular grooming also minimizes the hair wafting and floating through the house.

Animals don't perspire the way people do, and unless they make contact with dirt or smelly substances, they don't require frequent bathing. Most exhibitors spruce up a dog before a show and this often includes a bath. Pet owners who keep their dogs clean may only have to face that chore a couple of times a year, usually during the hair-shedding season.

Nails must be kept short for comfort. The inner quick, containing the nerves and blood vessels, grows with the nails and makes them more difficult to trim the longer they become. Long nails are unattractive (forbidden in a show dog) and can actually curl around to cut into the foot. Besides,

You are what you eat! Your Chow's health depends heavily on his diet.

Be careful when choosing treats for your Chow and never substitute them for a meal.

nails clicking on floors is annoying!

Clean your dog's ears every week or two by using a quality product obtained through a veterinarian or pet supply store. Or you can use baby oil and gauze. Owners of longhaired dogs often pluck the hair from the inner ear to help keep it clean and free of impacted wax. Medicated powder or ointment is recommended after pulling the hair.

A dog who shakes his head or rubs his ear may already have

The Chow who is accepted as a member of the family will enjoy a happy and healthy life.

earmites or an infection, which must be treated only by a prescribed otic medication. A red, inflamed or odorous ear also indicates a problem which should be treated by a vet.

DENTAL CARE

Dogs can't be fitted with dentures, so it's up to us to assure that their teeth last them as long as possible. Dry foods or a mixture of canned and dry help the teeth and gums remain healthy. Feeding only moist or canned dog food can allow food to stick around the gumline, causing gums to become inflamed or teeth to decay. Even with a diet of dry food, tartar (plaque) can accumulate.

Cleaning our dog's teeth with a veterinary dentifrice, or a mixture of baking soda and water, is suggested and should be done at least once a week. The act of rubbing with a toothbrush and/or cleaning plaque with a dental tool is more important than the product used.

In this area, as well as others, never substitute your own products for those specifically made for animals without asking a veterinarian. Human toothpaste or shampoos, for

Proper grooming is essential in preventing skin problems and flea infestation.

example, can actually be detrimental to his care.

PARASITES

Taking stool samples to the vet should be part of the annual examination or when observing symptoms such as diarrhea, bloody stools or worm segments. Dogs, especially puppies, may vomit and lose weight when infested with parasites.

A healthy red smooth-coated female at age eight weeks. Owner, Tim Malueg.

A good grooming table makes the proper care of your Chow's coat a simple and easy job.

Hookworms, roundworms, tapeworms, whipworms, coccidia and giardia are common. They can be eradicated with the proper medication but could be dangerous if left untreated. An over-the-counter drug may not be the right one for the particular parasite which your dog is harboring.

FLEAS

Bugs bug us and our pets. Fleas cause itching and carry

A number of commercial products can aid in the destruction and prevention of fleas and ticks. Photo courtesy of Hagen.

attempting to exterminate the pests, owners tear their hair, scratch their heads, chew their nails and are also miserable. Better to prevent than to cure, but for everyone's sanity, once the invasion has occurred, the sooner the evacuation, the better.

Talk to your veterinarian about the proper products to use, then arrange a regular reconnaissance to prevent a losing battle with fleas. During the warm months of the year, many people spray or powder animals (including other pets who may pass fleas to your dogs) once a week and

tapeworm eggs. The resultant scratching can irritate the skin so that rashes and hot spots develop. Dogs lose hair, scratch and chew at themselves and are miserable. In

A Chow Chow who spends a lot of time outside must be inspected carefully and on a regular basis for possible flea infestation.

premises (house and lawn) once a month. In between, owners keep up flea surveillance. At the slightest scratch, they look for telltale evidence—skittering teeny bugs or flea dirt, which looks like a sprinkling of pepper. It's usually easiest to see the freeloaders on the less hairy groin, belly or just above the root of the tail.

Among the products used to combat flea pests are dips, collars, powders, sprays, tags

You may want to apply a flea repellent spray to your Chow before taking him on an outdoor venture.

and internals—drops or pills. Instructions should be followed implicitly not only for best results, but because some of these products contain ingredients which may cause problems themselves if used carelessly.

If the critters are found, shampoo or dip all dogs (cats, too, with a product labeled safe for them), and spray living and sleeping quarters. It

Woods, pastures, and show grounds are all places where your Chow is likely to pick up fleas or ticks. You may want to inspect your Chow's coat when returning from such a trip.

doesn't do any good to treat the animal without debugging the environment or vice-versa. One flea who escapes will happily reinfest all over again. If the infestation is heavy, it may be necessary to fog your house and to repeat the procedure a few weeks later. All animals must be removed from the premises for the period of time specified on the fogger can.

In addition to the regular regime, many owners spray before walking dogs in areas where they are likely

Be especially careful with your Chow near grasses, trees, and shrubs, for these are the breeding grounds of the dangerous deer tick.

This Chow Chow is enjoying time outside in the Phillippines.

to pick them up, e.g., woods, pastures, training and show grounds. Most flea pesticides also kill ticks, and daily grooming sessions should include running your fingers through the dog's coat to find engorged ticks. Natural, non-insecticidal products can safely be used on a daily basis in the on-going war on fleas.

LYME DISEASE

One species of tick, *Ixodes scapularis*, the tiny deer tick, is the culprit which transmits the germ that causes Lyme disease to humans and animals. Deer ticks are found on mammals and birds, as well as in grasses, trees and shrubs. They are rarely visible because they are so small (as minute as the dot above an i), but the damage they can cause is magnified many times their size.

By running your fingers through your Chow's coat, you will be able to find and remove engorged fleas and ticks before they become a problem.

Examine your Chow carefully after excursions and see a doctor immediately if any symptoms of Lyme disease are apparent.

Here is Ch. Rebelruns Thunder Road as a healthy five month old pup.

Lyme disease can damage the joints, kidneys, heart, brain and immune system in canines and humans. Symptoms can include a rash, fever, lameness, fatigue, nausea, aching body and personality change among others. Left untreated, the disease can lead to arthritis, deafness, blindness, miscarriages and birth defects, heart disease and paralysis. It may prove to be fatal.

People should cover themselves with protective clothing while outdoors to prevent bites. Repellents are helpful for both dogs and humans. Examine the body after excursions and see a doctor if symptoms appear.

SKIN DISORDERS

Dogs, just like people, can suffer from allergies. While people most often have respiratory symptoms, dogs usually exhibit their allergies through itching, scratching, chewing or licking their irritated skin. These irritations often lead to angry, weeping "hot" spots.

Allergies are easy to detect but difficult to treat. Medications and topical substances can be useful, in addition to avoidance of the irritant, if possible.

CERF/OFA/VWD CERTIFICATION

Good breeders want to produce healthy,

Responsible Chow owners and breeders pay extra-special attention to the health of their dogs.

sound animals. The best way to do this is to start with healthy, normal animals judged to be free of hereditary conditions which can cause lameness, blindness and other disorders.

In the early years of dog shows, when symptoms of disease appeared, owners asked the opinion of experienced local breeders and veterinarians. As time went on, more specifics were learned about these various diseases and their heritability. Veterinarians took x-rays, performed blood tests and diagnosed symptoms. Now we

Good breeders start with normal animals who are free of impairing hereditary conditions. This healthy litter is six weeks old.

Healthy puppies which are clinically free of genetic disorders are easy to find, due in a large part to OFA certification.

are fortunate to have experts in various areas. Due to their specialized training and the numbers of cases these experts see, they are more likely to be accurate. Some have formed organizations which register clear animals and certify dogs free of hereditary disease.

Probably the first

organization of its type, the Orthopedic Foundation for Animals (OFA) certifies dogs free of hip dysplasia upon clearance of an x-ray by three board-certified radiologists. Dogs must be two years old for lifetime certification. The OFA also reads and gives opinions of radiographs with evidence of other heritable bone disorders such as craniomandibular osteopathy (CMO), osteochondritis

Make sure your bitch is OFA-cleared for hereditary diseases before you breed.

You should have your Chow's eyes examined for various diseases on a regular basis. This beautiful Chow has healthy clear eyes.

dessicans (OCD), ununited anchoneal process, Legg-Perthes disease and fragmented chronoid process. The organization's address is OFA, 2300 Nifong Blvd., Columbia, MO 65201.

Merry Christmas for two 12-week old Chow puppies.

Eye problems can be detected by veterinary opthalmologists available at teaching hospitals, private specialty practices (in larger cities) and at eye-screening clinics hosted by kennel clubs. These specialists examine for cataracts, entropion, pannus, retinal dysplasia, luxated lens, progressive retinal atrophy (PRA), central progressive retinal atrophy, Collie eye anomaly and other hereditary eye conditions. The Canine Eye Registration Foundation (CERF) may be contacted at CERF Veterinary Medicine Data Program, South Campus Courts, Bldg. C., Purdue University, West Lafayette, IN 47907. The age of the dog at first testing depends a great deal on the breed and the specific area of concern. A few diseases are apparent in puppyhood. CERF requires annual examination for certification of freedom from some diseases.

Von Willebrand's disease (VWD) is a bleeding disorder, similar to hemophilia. Clinical signs include lameness, aching joints, bloody stools, chronic bloody ear

The author winning with Ch. Cheries Jubilee of Rebelrun.

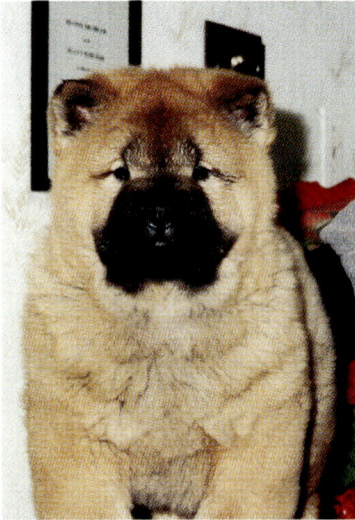

A number of diseases are apparent during puppyhood. Be sure to have your Chow fully checked by 6 months. Owner, Tim Malueg.

infections or a failure of the blood to clot. A blood test measures for adequate concentration of a specific clotting factor. Although it may be conducted in puppies as young as seven weeks, it should not be done within one month of vaccination; therefore, most are five or six months old. If a dog is in heat, has just whelped a litter or has been on antibiotics, the test should also be postponed for one month. Other disorders that are limited to just one or two breeds also have specific tests. Blood samples can be sent by your veterinarian to Dr. Jean Dodds, Veterinary Hematology Laboratory, Wadsworth Center for Laboratories and Research, NY State Dept. of Health, PO

Box 509, Albany, NY 12201-0509.

Before you breed, determine whether or not your dog is free of faulty pups. And they are certainly much less costly than a broken heart or a damaged reputation.

A Chow family portrait.

these and other hereditary diseases. Although the tests involve some cost, they are not as expensive as attempting to replace

BONE DISEASE

Many canine bone diseases have gained nicknames—albeit not affectionate—due to the unwieldy medical terminology. For

A black female smooth-coated puppy.

instance, canine cervical vertebral malformation/malarticulation syndrome is referred to as "wobbler" syndrome; panosteitis is shortened to pano; and canine hip dysplasia is often simply called CHD.

The first symptom is usually a limp. Diagnosis is made through a radiograph of the affected area.

Craniomandibular osteopathy (CMO) affects the growth of bone in the lower jaw, causing severe pain. Spondylosis is the

Ch. Lionheart Warrior, a top-winning Chow in the U.S.A. and Canada, at three years of age.

technical name for spinal arthritis.

Hip dysplasia is a poor fit of the hip joint into the socket, which causes erosion. Wobbler syndrome affects the neck vertebrae, causing weakness in the hindquarters and eventually the forequarters. Osteochondrosis dissecans (OCD) affects joints, most often the shoulder, elbow or stifle. Ununited anchoneal process, commonly referred to as elbow dysplasia, is a failure of the growth line to close, thereby creating

Rebelrun's Mountain Storm as a puppy.

Be sure to test your Chow for the various canine bone diseases, as these can be especially painful when left untreated. This healthy Chow male is one year old.

a loose piece in the joint. Kneecaps which pop out of the proper position are diagnosed as luxating patellas.

Legg-Perthes, most often seen in small breeds, is a collapsing of the hip joint. They all result in the same

This Chow is enjoying some quiet time in the snow.

thing: pain, lameness and, left untreated, arthritis.

The exception is pano, which is a temporary affliction causing discomfort during youth. Pano may be visible on x-rays, showing up as a cloudiness in the bone marrow in the long bones, particularly in fast-growing breeds.

EYES

Entropion is a condition in which the eyelid rolls inward. Eyelashes rub and irritate the cornea. In ectropion, the lower eyelid sags outward, allowing dirt to catch

Two Chows are better than one! Linda Bender poses with two of her favorite Chows.

in the exposed sensitive area and irritate the eye. In addition, extra eyelashes grow inside the lid which rub the surface of the eye and cause tearing. Either can be treated topically or, if severe, surgically.

ORGANIC DISEASE

Heart disease affects canines much as it does humans. A dog suffering from a problem involving the heart may exhibit weakness, fainting, difficult breathing, a persistent cough, loss of appetite, abdominal swelling due to fluid retention, exhaustion following normal exercise, or even heart failure and sudden death. Upon examination, an abnormal heart rhythm or sound or electrical potential might be detected, or changes in speed or strength noticed.

Treatment includes first stabilizing any underlying condition, followed by medications, low-sodium diet, exercise restriction and, possibly, surgery.

Chronic renal disease may first show up in vague symptoms—lethargy, diarrhea, anemia, weight loss and lack of appetite—as well as increased thirst and urination. Kidney disease is more common among geriatric canines. It

Rebelruns Teddy Mactyke with owner Eileen Bruington-Baldi.

Note the clear healthy eyes on this beautiful female Chow. Owners, Tony and Jean Larson.

may be compensated to some extent through diet. Diagnosis is most often made through blood and urine tests.

GASTRIC TORSION

Because a dog's stomach hangs like a hammock, the ends are effectively shut off if it flips over. Nothing can enter or exit. The normal bacterial activity in the stomach causes gas to build with no release through vomiting or defecating. The gas expands and, just like a balloon filled with helium, the stomach bulges and bloats.

It's physical torture for the dog and mental anguish for the owner who sees his dog moaning in agony and retching in a futile attempt to relieve the pressure.

With the veins and arteries to the

Ch. Rebelruns Southern Comfort at the age of two years.

stomach and spleen also closed off, shock sets in which can be rapidly fatal. Torsion—medically termed gastric dilatation and volvulus (GDV)—is an emergency. Experienced owners, particularly of large breeds, know there is no time to waste whether it's the middle of the night, a holiday or vacation time. It is urgent to reach a veterinarian who can treat the shock, followed by surgery to reposition the twisted organs. During surgery, the veterinarian may tack the stomach to the abdominal wall to prevent recurrence.

AUTO-IMMUNE DISEASES

Auto-immune disease, like cancer, is an umbrella term that includes many diseases of similar origin but showing different symptoms. Literally, the body's immune system views one of its own organs or tissues as foreign and launches an attack on it. Symptoms depend on which system is the target.

For instance, hypothyroidism symptoms can include lethargy, musty odor, temperament change, decreased fertility or unexplained weight gain, in addition to the more suggestive

The author wins with his Champion My-Sam's Knight in New York.

thin dry hair, scaliness of the skin, and thickness and darkening of the skin. Testing for hypothyroidism (which can be from causes other than auto-immune disease) may be conducted as early as eight to twelve months, using the complete blood count, blood chemistry, thyroid T4, T3 and free T4 tests.

Rheumatoid arthritis is a result of an auto-immune reaction to the joint surfaces. The resulting inflammation and swelling causes painful deformed joints. If the red blood cells are perceived as foreign invaders and destroyed, the rapid onset anemia (called auto-immune hemolytic anemia) can cause collapse and death if diagnosis and treatment are not quickly initiated. Often an auto-immune reaction in an organ causes destruction of that organ with subsequent loss of function. Auto-immune disease of the adrenal gland leads to hypoadrenocortissism (Addison's disease.)

The same reaction in the thyroid gland soon has the dog exhibiting symptoms of hypothyroidism. Auto-immune diseases of the skin are called pemphigus, while those of connective tissue are termed lupus. Many other varieties exist, and each requires specialized testing and biopsy. Most respond to treatment once a diagnosis is made.

EPILEPSY

Probably because of the feeling of

Ch. Sonlit Yang Fu of Pycoe, owned by Sandy Pynn.

Ch. Rebelruns Back on Track at home with Bruce and Annette Rathbun.

helplessness, one of the most frightening situations a dog owner can face is watching a beloved dog suffer seizures. As in people, epilepsy is a neurological condition which may be controlled by anticonvulsant drugs. Many breeds of dogs have a hereditary form of epilepsy usually with an adult onset.

The University of Pennsylvania Canine Epilepsy Service has conducted studies of drugs and dosages, their efficacy and long-term side effects, to assist veterinarians in prescribing anticonvulsants.

ALTERNATIVE TECHNIQUES

During the 1970s and '80s, acupuncture, chiropractic and holistic medicine became part of the canine health picture. Veterinarians who have received special

A healthy, handsome Chow male relaxes on his grooming platform.

training in these fields now practice their techniques on patients who do not respond to or cannot take previously prescribed medical treatments. Patients have responded favorably to these methods, especially when done in conjunction with medical supervision. Certainly, when it comes to a much-loved animal, the most recent up-to-date techniques should be tried before resorting to euthanasia.

Owners should be aware, however, that practitioners must have a veterinary degree to practice on animals and that the holistic, chiropractic and acupunctural treatment should not take the place of standard veterinary medicine, but enhance it.

GERIATRICS

As dogs age, problems are more likely to occur, just as they do in their human counterparts. It is even more important to examine your dogs, noting every "normal" lump and sag, so that if a new one occurs you are aware. Owners should make appointments for veterinary check-ups at least once a year.

Elderly canines suffer the same infirmities as we do

This gorgeous Chow is from Sonlit.

Chows suffer from the same aging problems as humans, and need yearly checkups. Here Rebelruns Thunder Buns plays in the snow.

when we age. Deafness, arthritis, cancers, organ disease and loss of vision are common. Symptoms such as a cough, bloating, weight loss, increased water consumption and a dry thin coat are warning signs to seek medical attention. Many aging patients can be made comfortable and sustain a quality life.

Although our dogs will never live long enough to satisfy us, we can extend their lives through our precautions, specialized nutrition, exercise and routine veterinary care.

EMERGENCIES

The get-your-vet-on-the-phone-drive-there-as-quickly-as-is-safe emergency situations are few, thankfully. But they do occur, and that's why all owners should be aware of symptoms. Veterinarian numbers for day and night calls should be posted prominently near the phone.

Occasions that are well worth a middle-of-the-night payment are: shock, anoxia (choking), dystocia (labor and whelping complications), hemorrhage, gastric torsion, electric shock, large wounds, compound fractures and heat stroke. In addition, neurological symptoms such as paralysis, convulsions and unconsciousness indicate an emergency. If your dog has ingested poison, been severely burned or hit by a car, for instance, call an emergency number for help.

EUTHANASIA

Most owners dread facing the decision of euthanizing a pet. But as hard as it is to make that decision and drive a beloved animal on his final journey, it is more difficult to watch a dog who has lost all quality of life struggle through a day-to-day fog of pain. Of course, it's also more stressful for the animal, and don't we love him enough to spare him that trauma? Certainly, eyes that plead "Help me" deserve a humane response.

Euthanasia is a fact that most breeders and pet owners must eventually face if they do not wish their animals to suffer. Ask your veterinarian to administer a non-lethal anesthetic or tranquilizer, literally putting the dog to sleep while you hold your pet and caress him gently. The dog will drift off to sleep peacefully and without fear, no longer suffering. At that point, the veterinarian injects a lethal overdose of anesthesia which instantly stops the heart. Death truly comes as a servant in peace; euthanasia is a kind, quiet death.

Arrangements should be made for the disposition of the body prior to the euthanasia. Some owners wish to bury the remains themselves (be aware of local regulations, however, which are becoming more stringent) or to have the dog cremated. Others want the veterinarian to handle the arrangements. Planning ahead saves more difficult

Joyce Balbontin proudly wins with "Zeus," her beautiful Chow male.

decisions during the trauma of losing your friend.

VETERINARY SPECIALISTS

With a surplus of small animal veterinarians expected in the latter part of the 20th century, and a surging volume of knowledge and medical technology, many veterinary school graduates elect to specialize with additional courses and training. These include surgery, dentistry, oncology, radiology, neurology, cardiology, dermatology,

Two Chow Champion males waiting at a dog show.

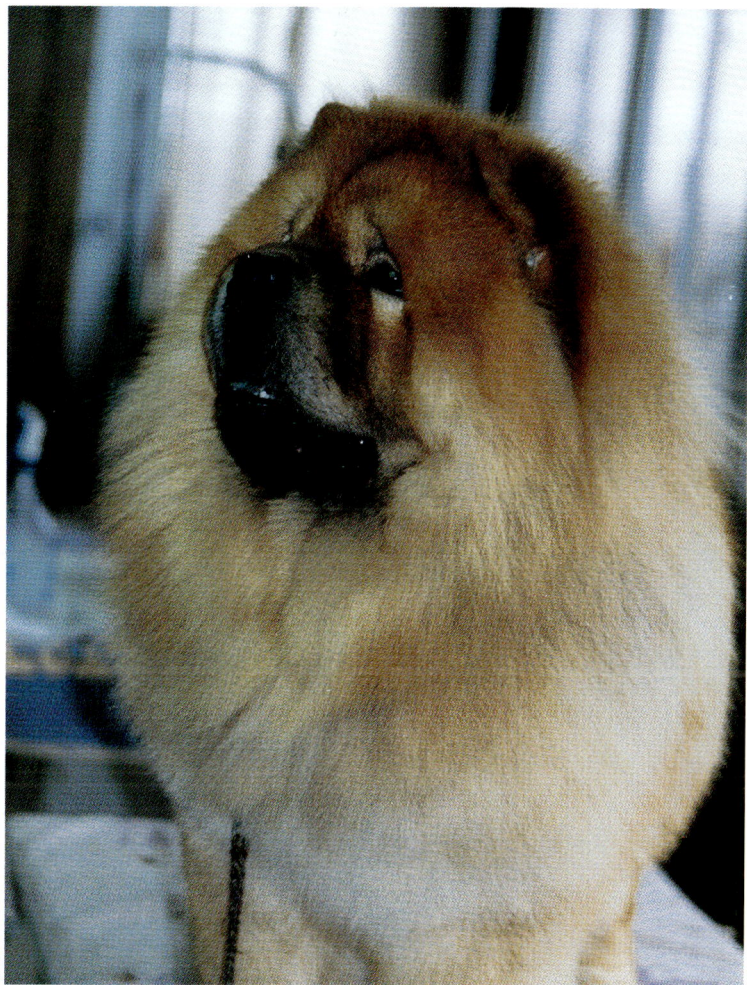

A young male Ch. My-Sam's Knight in New York displays beautiful dark eyes and a shiny coat.

Dynasty Chows' Rebelrun Jack Daniels poses boastfully for a portrait.

ophthalmology, theriogenology (reproduction) and internal medicine.

This "overpopulation," naturally, is a boon to pet lovers. If your dog has one of these problems, your veterinarian may refer you to a board-certified specialist or contact one for advice on specialized treatment. Any concerned, caring veterinarian will be happy to do so and assist his patient to live a healthier, fuller life.

Everyone who owns dogs for very long begins to build a canine medical chest. Basic supplies should include cotton, gauze, tweezer, ipecac, muzzle, styptic powder, cotton swabs, rectal thermometer, petroleum jelly, hydrogen peroxide, ear medication, anti-diarrhea preparation, ibuprofin pain killer and one-inch adhesive tape. Include first aid instructions and a poison help sheet with a hotline number.

ETHICS

In all diseases, symptoms may vary from mild to severe. In the most extreme cases, victims may have to be euthanized. Many do live, however, under veterinary care and supervision, occasional medication and owner TLC. Nevertheless, it's important to know which disease are known to be inherited. Our dogs can carry the factors which transmit hereditary conditions and pass on their afflictions to a higher than normal percentage of their progeny. Affected dogs should be spayed or neutered and never allowed to transmit their discomfort to future generations. Owners should also be aware that AKC regulations specify that surgically corrected dogs may not compete in the breed ring.

A very merry Christmas at the home of Dave and Pat Foose and their Pendleton Chows.

Chows age gracefully and continue to win at dog shows. This is BIS and BISS Can-Am. Ch. Lionheart Warrior at age five. Owner, G. Forsythe.

Am. Ch. Rebelrun's Southern Comfort, bred and owned by the authors, is a multiple group winning Chow Chow male.

Canine Behavior

Canines have the same individual traits and quirks that people do. Each one is different. Although certain breeds have predispositions to the behavior elicited by their instincts and breed nature, every single dog must be judged as an individual.

Every breed was developed for a particular purpose. The best at doing their jobs were selectively kept and bred. Those that did not perform as they were supposed to were usually culled or, occasionally, given away as pets. The nature of the beast is predetermined by its ancestors—and by the people who bred them.

Breeders chose hounds who followed their talented noses, trailed the game and told their owners about it in rich, full voice, once the quarry was found. Other hounds were lean and fast, with the inborn urge and ability to run and chase prey by sight. Hunters wanted sporting dogs with

Clif and Linda Bender's Chows at play.

stamina, persistence and the ability to work in various terrains and climes. Working breeds had to be large enough to haul a heavy burden and protective enough to ward off intruders. Shepherds wanted assistance in gathering their flocks and herds, so they called upon herding dogs. Northern people needed a dog who could withstand the cold, pull sleds and perhaps round up the reindeer. And in every group, dogs were miniaturized, kept and adored for nothing other than their sweet demeanor, winsome looks and companionship. Yet, they still have the modern traits of their larger forebears.

The instinctive breed natures that our ancestors selected for, chose and developed can be the very behavior trait which drives today's owners nuts. Along with the loyalty, stamina, speed, strength, sensitivity, intelligence and protective qualities came chasing (cars, not cattle), digging (in flower beds instead of fox burrows) killing (birds in lieu of rats), straying instead of hunting, displaying misplaced aggression against the "trespassing" mail carrier, and barking/yapping/howling/baying/yelping, usually at the wrong time.

When we, as dog owners, understand our pet's natural inclinations, we can decide which traits we can tolerate and which are unacceptable for our lifestyle and home. Then, steps can be

Ch. Rebelruns Knight of My-Sam at a dog show.

taken to avoid the intolerable and to train our pet to exhibit desirable behavior and be a good canine citizen.

TRAINING

Instruction begins at home, the minute we introduce our pup to his new quarters. In the beginning, it seems as though every other word is "No," just as when we are running after a human toddler. But, eventually, we can attempt various other

Ch. Rebelruns Starlite Knight waiting for his master to come home.

Blonds and Chows go together!

preschool lessons: "sit" for a treat, "lie down" while brushing, "stand" for pretty, "stay" for a split second, "outside" for potty, and so on. The dog's vocabulary will increase though yours seems to have regressed. Before you know it, you will need to expand his education and yours.

Most large communities have dog clubs or individuals that offer training classes. People who live in smaller towns or more rural areas may have to search a bit, but can often find trainers within a half-hour's drive. The time spent at classes is well worth the effort.

A good instructor has seen every problem in the book and then some and can give you the benefit of his experience. Someone has always walked in your—and your dog's—footprints, no matter how annoying, embarrassing or frustrating.

Obedience schools usually require that a dog should be six months old or close to it. But there are other alternatives for early socializing and education. Puppy "kindergarten" is fun for everyone, dogs and people alike. Nothing is cuter than a pup, (except a bunch of pups) bouncing, bobbling and *boinnng*ing about. Even the most experienced owner is set back in finesse, while working with a wiggleworm, trying to avoid stepping on paws and encouraging acceptable puppy manners. Lessons range from sit, stand and stay (for the vet) to nail clipping, basic grooming, walking on leash and coming on command. It's fun and amazing how quickly these youngsters grow, from the tiniest Chihuahua to a mighty Great Dane, and before anyone realizes, it's time to go on to a higher level of education.

"OSO," dressed for the holiday season, is an excellent house dog.

Conformation classes often accept puppies as soon as their basic inoculation schedule is in effect, or at about eight weeks of age. Training for the breed ring consists of walking and trotting on leash. The pup learns to stand and allow the "judge" to pet him all over, look in his mouth and examine his testicles. Tips to aspiring handlers are given as well, allowing us to get our feet wet before diving into the big pond of dog shows.

Two well trained Chows take top honors in the costume contest!

Chow Chows love to play in the snow.

Training for the show ring begins when your Chow is a puppy.

Class training, whether obedience, conformation or kindergarten, teaches the owners how to become and remain the leader in this twosome. Just like a good dance team, one leads and the other follows. Unless we want a dog who demands us to fetch and cater to his every whim, we'd better learn to lead.

Instructors inform enrollees about the type of leash and collar to use, but most suggest a chain link or "slip" collar, with a leather leash. Probably 90 percent of the class simply wants a pet who doesn't jump up on everybody who comes to the door or can walk to the corner without tripping his owner. Class instruction includes basic obedience routines, however, so that the person who wishes to show his dog can do so competitively.

Obedience exercises include heeling (on and off leash), standing, sitting, staying, lying down and coming when called. All of us can take advantage of those handy commands even if we never set foot in a ring.

How nice it is to tell a dog "Down" just as he jumps up to greet us with muddy paws or to say "Stand, stay" so that the veterinarian can examine him.

WHAT MAKES YOUR DOG TICK?

Canine body language can tell us what the intentions of the animal are and how we can greet the dog. A bow with tail wagging is an invitation to play.

Submission to your will is shown by a lowered head, slinking movement and ears laid back against the skull. In extreme, the dog may lie down, roll over on his back or even urinate. Fear is demonstrated by a tucked tail, backing up, showing teeth and growling or barking. An aggressive dog stands as tall as possible, head high, tail raised, up on toes, ears and hackles raised, teeth

A young Chow puppy makes friends with a llama.

Chow Chows make great lap dogs. Cindy Durman and Rebelruns Jack Daniels.

bared, tense and growling.

CHEWING

Again, crating when there is no supervision prevents rather than cures. Bitter Apple™, which can be found at a pet supply store, is an excellent deterrent, however, as is tabasco sauce or liquid red pepper. Supply plenty of acceptable chew toys, such as Nylafloss®,

hambone scented

GUMABONE

POOCH PACIFIER

SAVES
MONEY &
DOGS' LIVES

PLAY TOY
& EXERCISER

LASTS 10 TIMES
LONGER THAN
RAWHIDE

SOUPER SIZE

For Large Dogs

"WHY"
On Reverse
Side
!

GUMABONE *Pooch Pacifier*®
NYLABONE CORP., P.O. Box 27 Neptune City, N.J. 07753

Annealed nylon and polyurethane chew toys such as the Gumabone® are recommended by veterinarians as proven-safe and effective canine chew devices.

Nylabones®, and other "pooch pacifiers."

BARKING

This annoying canine communication may be the hardest habit to break, because it is ingrained in most creatures to create noise. After all, it's so handy, the noisemaker is right under our noses! Can you imagine a life without using your vocal cords?

Discouraging this neighbor-irritant is difficult if a chronic barker is the evil-doer. In those situations, it might be easier to buy the neighbor earplugs, or a good bottle of wine or his own noisemaker! But if the problem is serious, electronic bark collars or debarking surgery are preferable to poisoning or shooting. Confining the dog indoors, particularly at night, can be a solution. Most people object more strenuously to nighttime howling, yapping or yodeling, and who can blame them?

A monotonous lifestyle can be the cause of the canine complaints. Give your dog something to do or wear him out, so that he sleeps instead of baying at the moon . . . or sun . . . or birds. Listen to what your dog is saying.

Even Chow Chow puppies enjoy the Easter Bunny!

Index

*Page numbers in **boldface** refer to illustrations.*
All titles have been removed from dogs' names for reader's convenience.

A
Aging, 64
American Kennel Club, 8, 87, 90
AKC, 8, 87, 90

B
Balbontin, Joyce, **225**
Barking, 248
Bearden's Mountain Man, **143**
Bone diseases, 204
Breeding, 127–132
Bruington-Baldi, Eileen, **211**

C
Canine Eye Registration Foundation, 201
CERF, 201
Cherie's Jubilee of Rebelrun's, **6**, **126**, **141**, **156**, **201**

Chewing, 247
Chewing, 247
Chowlamar's Ravishing Ruby, **140**
Coat, 9, 77, 120
Conformation, 141–148
Crates, 30–32, 47, 59, **60**

D
Deer tick, 191–192
Diet, 163
Distemper, 172
Durman, Cindy, **247**
Dysplasia, 125–127

E
Ears, 81
Epilepsy, 218
Euthanasia, 168, 223–226
Exercise, 163
Eyes, 79–81, 200, 208

F
Feeding, 35
Feet, 81
Fleas, 185–191
Foose, Dave and Pat, **230**

G
Gastric torsion, 212
Grooming, 178–181

H
Haleakala No Ruff Stuff, **100**
Hank of Rebelrun's, **173**
Hawke, Joshua, **22**
Hawke, Rachael, **22**, **42**
Heart disease, 210
Hip dysplasia, 206

I
Imagine The Duke, **169**
Ixodes scapularis, 191

J
Jonel's Track

Mactavish, **115**, **126**, **156**

L
Legg-Perthes, 207
Lionheart Warrior, **205**, **231**
Lionheart Whirlwind, **170**
Lov-Chow's Risen Star, **1**
Lyme disease, 191–195

M
Microchip identification, 49–50
Mishika Sweetpea of Rebelrun's, **122**
My-Sam's Knight in New York, **80**, **215**, 227

N
Neutering, 132–133

O
Obedience, 150–152
—exercises, 245
OCD, 206

OFA, 123–125, 198
Orthopedic Foundation for Animals, 123–125, 198
Osteochondrosis dissecans, 206
Overheating, 49

P
Parasites, 184
Parvovirus, 173
Pedigree, 145

R
Rebelrun's Amberosia, **149**, 158
Rebelrun's Annabelle Li, **166**
Rebelrun's Bacardi, **89**
Rebelrun's Back On Track, **63**, **218**
Rebelrun's Bobby Dazzler, **12**
Rebelrun's Call to Glory, **21**, **174**
Rebelrun's Dark Oracle, **11**, **69**, **109**

Rebelrun's Dreamer for Sal Mae, **145**
Rebelrun's Garfield, **103**
Rebelrun's Honeybunch, **71**
Rebelrun's Jack Daniels, **68**, **228**, **247**
Rebelrun's Jenny Linn, **157**
Rebelrun's Jessica, **147**
Rebelrun's Johnny B Goode, **3**
Rebelrun's Knight of My-Sam, **235**
Rebelrun's Mountain Storm, **206**
Rebelrun's Peppermint Twist, **123**
Rebelrun's Red Alert, **85**
Rebelrun's Sir Tavish, **98**
Rebelrun's Southern Comfort, **86**, **213**, **232**

Rebelrun's Starlite Knight, **236**

Rebelrun's Stratofortress, **116**, **142**, **151**, **168**

Rebelrun's Teddy MacTyke, **134**, **165**, **211**

Rebelrun's The Californian, **132**, **153**

Rebelrun's Thunder Buns, **222**

Rebelrun's Thunder Road, **194**

Redcloud Sylvan Eden's Tale, **107**, **125**, **154**

Rhapsody's Mister Big Shot, **13**, **162**

Rheumatoid arthritis, 216

Ridgecrest The Floridian, **46**

Rob-Loi Emperor of Rebelrun's, **135**

S

Skin disorders, 195

Socialization, 64–67, 134–138

Sonlit All The Tea in China, **105**

Sonlit Haiku, **93**

Sonlit Imagine the Duke, **10**

Sonlit Yang Fu, **217**

Spaying, 132–133

Standard, 87–116

Sunny Oaks Dream Seekers Lena, **106**

T

Taibel Texas Tiger of Ukwong, **7**

Teeth, 84, 182–183

Training, 68–70, 236–245

Traveling, 46

V

Vaccination, 176

Veterinarian, 45

Von Willebrand's disease, 201–202

W

Wobbler syndrome, 206

More Chow Chow books from T.F.H.

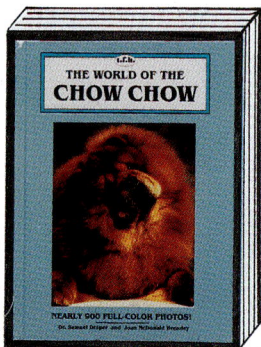

The World of the Chow Chow
TS-149, 526 pp.

The long-anticipated companion to the authors' best-selling The Book of the Chow Chow, **The World of the Chow Chow** is an unprecedented, nation-wide celebration of the Chow Chow, complete with nearly 900 full-color photographs, plus almost 100 historical black-and-whites, practical information for both the devoted fancier and the freshly bitten newcomer, and vital statistics updating Chow events and developments to the present day. The sheer abundance of photography, illustrating champions of today and yesterday at home—in the ring, in obedience competitions—makes this extraordinary volume a reliable source for all breeders and fanciers

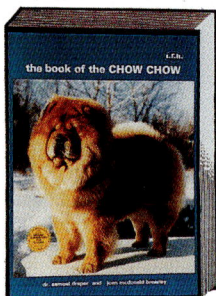

The Book of the Chow Chow
H-965, 576 pp.

The Book of the Chow Chow by Dr. Samuel Draper and Joan McDonald Brearley is for anyone who is interested in the ChowChow or its history in any way. This massive and exhaustively detailed book is the perfect reference volume

The Chow Chow
PS 812, 288 pp.

The Chow Chow covers every area of interest to owners of Chow Chows. Noted author/judge Anna Katherine Nicholas provides a world of fascination and valuable knowledge about this revered oriental breed

All-Breed Books from T.F.H. Publications, Inc.

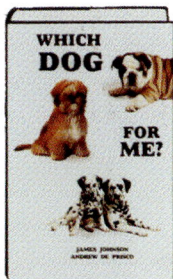

KW-227, 96 pp. 100 color photos.

SK-044, 64 pp. Over 50 color photos.

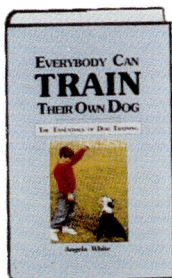

TW-113, 256 pp. 200 color photos.

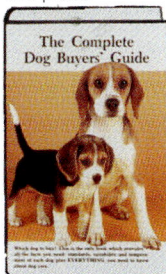

H-1061, 608 pp. 100 B&W photos.

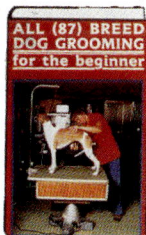

TS-101, 192 pp. Over 100 photos.

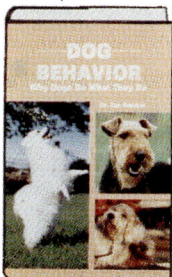

H-1016, 224 pp. 135 photos.

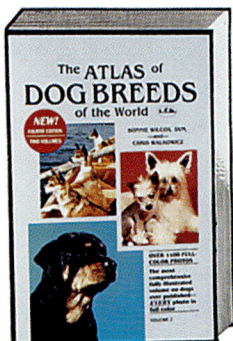

H-1091, 2 Vols., 912 pp.
Over 1100 color photos.

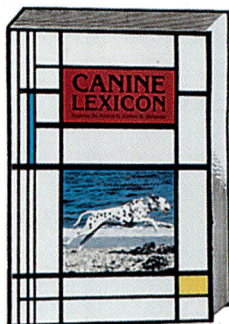

TS-175, 896 pp.
Over 1300 color photos.

TS-220, 64 pp.

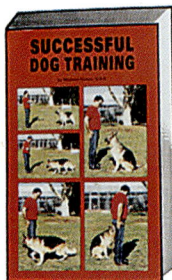

TS-205, 156 pp.
Over 130 color photos.

H-1106, 544pp.
Over 400 color photos.

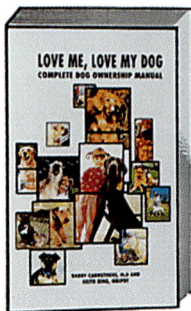

TS-212, 256 pp.
Over 140 color photos.

TS-220, 64 pp.